P9-DIY-591

LOOKING

for

SIGNS

LOOKING

for

SIGNS

Essays and Columns

By DIANE CAMERON

Looking for Signs
Copyright © 2012 by Diane Cameron

All rights reserved. No part of this book may be used or reproduced in any form, electronic or mechanical, including photocopying, recording, or scanning into any information storage and retrieval system, without written permission from the author except in the case of brief quotation embodied in critical articles and reviews.

Cover design by Jenny Kemp
Book design by Jenny Kemp

Printed in the United States of America

The Troy Book Makers • Troy, New York • thetroybookmakers.com

To order additional copies of this title, contact your favorite local bookstore or visit www.tbmbooks.com

ISBN: 978-1-61468-125-0

For my husband, David John Pascone,

with love and gratitude.

Introduction

The title of this collection comes from the lead essay, "Looking for Signs," which I wrote in 1999 as a holiday piece for the Albany Times Union. The first time that I read T.S. Eliot's poem, Journey of the Magi, I knew I was home. Someone else had understood this risk of writing, of creating, of living. He wrote,

> At the end we preferred to travel all night,
> Sleeping in snatches,
> With the voices singing in our ears saying,
> That this was all folly.

My life has always felt like that. And all of my life I have prayed for signs.

For years my family told the story of how I began to write before I knew how to write. I had a kind of made-up cursive writing—all swirls and dashes—and I "wrote" stories and even a "newspaper" in my toddler typeface. I understand now that this was not so farfetched for a little girl who saw her parents reading four newspapers a day. They talked about what was "in the paper" all the time. I grasped what mattered and how to create it for myself.

But what went unsaid was how to make a creative life. I always wanted --and perhaps still do want –to have clear signs to direct my life's work. I have read bubble gum fortunes and played with Ouija Boards, and I have wished for skywriting or an envelope from God with my name on it that contained a note saying, "Diane, here's what you should do."

What I see now is that during all those years of wondering about, and suffering over, what to do when I grew up, is that I had always been writing. My vocation was hiding in plain sight.

The other thing that was always part of me, but again hidden right in front of me, was that I cared deeply about what makes people tick. What is it that makes us good or bad, happy or scared or...

That pondering is an inescapable part of me. Why? Why? Yes, the toddler again. I wanted to know how people came to be the way they were. There were very compelling and heartbreaking reasons that I was trying to figure out the people closest to me-- my brothers, my mother, my father (you'll find all of them in these essays)--but I was also trying to figure out myself. What did I want and why did I want it? What did I feel, and how had that come to be?

I am still doing that. And I'm still following breadcrumbs and stars and footprints and ideas. Those journeys are here in these essays. No, I haven't made a living from writing. But I have made a life.

Looking for Signs

I laugh at how many times I have prayed for a sign to let me know that I was on the right path or to help me make a choice. In difficult moments I have begged for skywriting or an envelope from God with my name on it. Maybe I watched too many episodes of Mission Impossible growing up, but part of me wants instructions from a higher power that clearly spell out what I should do with my life.

I know God doesn't work that way, but I know I'm not alone in wanting him to. Some people flip coins or watch birds or follow the crude metals index. Others go to Tarot readers, throw the I Ching and keep psychics in business.

Years ago when people close to me were dying and I tearfully demanded to know God's will, a friend more experienced in grief chastised and reassured me by saying, "Gods will is what is." That simplicity silenced me for a while.

But I come back again to wanting to know and it's often at this time of year. There's a good reason. As the winter begins and we are faced with dark and cold there is a pull from deep in our bones that makes us seek light and answers.

The need for light at this time of year is so great that we have adapted culturally to give it to ourselves. We've had Hanukkah, now Solstice, and soon Christmas: all stories about finding light.

The part of the Christmas story that means the most to me is that of the three wise men making their journey, traveling on a hunch, a belief, and their deep wanting. They had studied the sky for years and then they saw their sign. The star in the east led them to the baby Jesus.

In his poem, Journey of the Magi T.S. Eliot wrote: "At the end we preferred to travel all night/ sleeping in snatches/ with the voices singing in our ears/that this was all folly."

Of course that is the problem with star following. You just don't know. We see this most painfully looking at the news. Stories of young men and women as heroes and others, the same age, who commit terrible crimes. Perhaps all following their stars. But how do you know until you show up whether there's going to be a baby or a bullet?

We have to remember that the wise men did more than follow stars. Each one packed up his gift: the gold, frankincense and myrrh, and gave it.

So the wise men's lesson is about faith: We study, we consult with others, we try to be wise men and women, but then we have to get on our camels, bring the gifts and hope we are doing good.

This is solstice week and these are our darkest days. There are many scary things in front of us: global warming, a war with no end in sight and the daily crimes committed against our hearts.

We cope in the most ancient of ways. We go toward the light--to neon and to the crowds at the mall just as our ancient relatives were drawn to the stars and the fire.

Through all of this we'll read our horoscopes. We'll hope our loved ones will be spared the only thing that no one can be, which is death. We'll look at the night sky and try to believe. No wonder a baby born in a barn is a great story. No wonder we look for signs.

Up, Up and Away

The airline industry is under fire again. Passengers want more flights, better connections and lower fares, and yes, more security measures. I listen to the criticisms and I shake my head.

The past few months I have been in a lot of airplanes and consequently lots of airports. Each time, as I await my boarding call, I take up my usual position with my nose pressed against the windows near at the gate. It's almost always me and a group of six-year-old boys watching the planes taxi, take off and land. We oooh and aaah as we assess each plane's trajectory. The adults behind us are reading newspapers and fuming about the delay. It's one of those times that I'm certain kids are smarter than adults.

I have a fantasy that someday I'll be brave enough to walk over and take away the newspapers and laptops and say, "You have no idea what's going on here." Here's what adults miss about flying: A lot of people get in a big metal box and by moving that box very fast something called "lift" occurs. It's pretty much a freak of physics—air rushing at two different speeds forces an adjustment in space—and the big box full of people goes up in the air. This metal box travels at 500 miles per hour traversing thousands of miles over land and water and then it comes back down with hardly a bump 99.9 percent of the time.

Modern airplanes are, after all, the safest means of travel available. We are in greater danger on the expressway than the folks flying overhead.

For most of my life I have been in love with airplanes. Years ago I learned to fly so I could do it myself. I've memorized the explanation for airfoils, wind speed and drag, but I still think it's a miracle every time a plane takes off.

Not long ago on a flight from Pittsburgh I felt redeemed. In the seat behind me a little boy was watching the takeoff from his window seat. As the physical sensations merged with his visual confirmation that we were airborne, he let loose a laugh that rolled from the center of his being. It was the wisest and happiest laugh I have ever heard.

Yes, we're Americans: we're important and in a hurry. But we miss so much when we live that emotional posture. We claim to love nature but we miss the fact that aerodynamics is part of nature. Air and metal and physics are an amazing combination when they make an airplane fly.

An article last year in the Atlantic Monthly predicted not bigger or faster commercial planes but a system of aviation based on small planes and smaller airports. I'm thrilled to consider a future where we can drive a short distance, skip waiting in lines, and grab one of 10 available seats to get where we're going. By taking advantage of the network of smaller airports—and moving away from the big airline hubs—we'll achieve faster, safer and easier travel.

Often friends, who know my love of planes and flying, will say sheepishly, "Oh you must think I'm silly to be afraid of flying." But I don't. A certain amount of fear is the respect due to this phenomenon and it's an intuitive acknowledgment of what is happening when an airplane goes—and stays—up.

While a plane can fly because it obeys several simultaneous rules of physics, watch what happens if you drop your pen or this newspaper. It will go down; gravity is a force to be respected.

Yes, I know the delays are miserable and there's no more food, but this summer, when you fly, and you find yourself waiting, come and join me and the kids at the window. We'll be watching the planes take off and marveling at part of the natural world so often taken for granted.

In Defense of Late Shoppers

Today—December 20th--is one of my favorite days of the year. This afternoon I'll head out to start my Christmas shopping. For a long time I was ashamed to admit that I prepared for the holidays with less than a week to go, but the truth is, this is my favorite part of Christmas.

No, I didn't procrastinate. I well know the advice about how to make Christmas shopping easier. But there are some things that don't get better just by being easier. I've read many of those How to Get Organized books, but I've also lived through enough tragedy to know that trying to organize one's life is an illusion.

I grant you that there will be a moment this week when I'll envy those who had their gifts wrapped in August. But that's kind of like having a good report from the dentist, isn't it? All very wholesome, but where's the fun?

And don't get me started on the people who buy everything online. How much holiday spirit does that take? Yes you meet the technical requirement of gift given—but then why not just hand everyone a twenty-dollar bill, and say, "Hey, have a go at it"?

I also hate that suggestion that you should keep a stash of generic gifts on hand in case someone surprises you with a gift and you were not prepared to reciprocate. That's just mean. Someone was just about to feel generous and you cut them off at the knees with a retaliatory box of bath salts. It's the cruelest one-upmanship.

Those of us who begin our shopping this week will enjoy the real spirit of Christmas: we get to watch humanity test itself and we'll see kindness and patience and grace enacted –or honored in the breach--in toy stores and next to the stack of 30% off cashmere cardigans. We will also endure the "I was done in August" folks who just learned they need one more thing; they will typically be the ones cutting in line or sighing heavily and making lots of eye contact, wanting everyone to share their misery.

No, we who start our shopping now are engaging in a holiday ritual much closer to the original: It's cold out, traffic is as slow as a lane of donkeys, there is no room in the parking lot, and we get to watch a young family with a triple stroller searching the mall for a baby changing area. It makes you want to drop to your knees and pray.

Yes, shopping in August could make Christmas nice and tidy. But real life is anything but that. Consider the story of the Holy Family: There was no advance plan; Mary was days away from delivering a baby; then they went on a long trip, and she had to give birth in a barn. Not tidy and neat.

The crux of that first Christmas is that sometimes in the midst of mess and stress, angels show up and miracles happen.

But in order to experience that you have to be willing to join the fray and put yourself where human beings are being human. Yes, it's a gamble, but relationships are like casinos: You must be present to win.

So this week I'll be where humanity is. I'm heading out to the mall, bundled up, grinning and bracing myself for mixed encounters with my fellow man.

I'll be trekking in from the outer loop of the parking lot, looking for a few gifts and the real spirit of Christmas.

The Best Beach Book in the World

We are sliding into the final third of summer. From here we push on to the finish line at Labor Day. The wish lists we made in June weigh on us: the outings, the visitors, trips, chores, projects and for many the pile of books we promised we'd read this summer.

Each friend's recommendation and each review adds another book to our pile. Our motivations are good; we want to grow and better understand ourselves and the world around us. The books pile up on the coffee table and the bed stand, and our library list is dog-eared and scribbled. Even worse there are new categories. There's more "Chick Lit" and new graphic novels too, each offering more literary ways of seeing the world. Then, too, many of us have our ongoing side list of "issues" we're working on: parenting or relationship skills. That comes with more books to read.

So, where to begin? You'd like a good novel and a romance and some history too. You want some help with the relationship thing, and, these days, you want a better understanding of politics and economics. But then there is also that stack of business books you saved all year; you want some new ideas about management and to think about work differently.

But with four weeks to go maybe you just throw up your hands and go to the movies. If there's not going to be enough time to read it all anyway, how do you choose?

I have the answer. There is one book that you can read now that will give you everything you're wishing and hoping for. It is the one and only book you need for the boat and tote, the chaise lounge, the blanket or the bed.

Hands-down, the single best summer book is Anna Karenina by Leo Tolstoy. With Tolstoy's tale you get everything in one: romance, history, a relationship how-to book, and the best management advice you'll ever read.

Now, don't balk at the bulk. Yes, it's a big book but by choosing Anna K. you only have to buy one book. Here's why:

Anna K. is the best relationship book ever written. It's got examples of how to make a marriage work and how to how to ruin one from the start. Worried about infidelity? This is the book that, well, wrote the book on that topic. Tolstoy shows how couples get into that terrain and how you can get back out. Robin Norwood's famous Women Who Love Too Much doesn't even come close to what Tolstoy writes about emotional dependency and the impact of addiction on a family.

As for new ideas about work: Tolstoy offers the most compelling and insightful analysis of why people work, and how to motivate them. Tom Peters has written half a dozen books trying to get at what Tolstoy packs into just a few scenes. Levin, Anna's cousin, is the best management consultant you could hire; by showing us Levin in the field with his workers, Tolstoy articulates the subtleties of the relationship between worker and manager, and shows exactly how you can make a day's work good or bad.

But, you may insist, fiction can't help your real life. With all due respect, you're wrong. When we read "to escape," it's not from life but to life. Fiction gives us the assurance that the story that we love most—our own—is worthy.

Besides, if you finish Anna K. before August runs into fall, there's always Tolstoy's other little book, War and Peace, which brings us right back to this day and our very, very real lives.

Babar — Au Revoir Cécile

It has been said that behind every successful man is a woman. It turns out that behind the world's most successful elephant there is also a woman to be thanked.

Even now, as some cast a disdainful eye toward all things French, there is one Frenchman who remains untouched by criticism and who may even be the kind of leader we need now. He is, of course, the French ruler, politician, and diplomat: the elephant Babar.

Just a few weeks ago, at age 99, Cécile de Brunhoff, the woman behind the elephant, died. Cécile created Babar as a bedtime story for her children. Her husband Jean wrote down the stories and illustrated the first Babar book, which was published in 1931. Jean did try to credit Cécile, but she had her name removed before the book was printed. Jean de Brunhoff died in 1937, and Babar's adventures continue to be illustrated by Laurent de Brunhoff, Cécile and Jean's oldest son.

Most people meet Babar when they are young, but I didn't meet him until I was much older. The introduction was a gift from a friend when I was going through a bad time. I keep a picture of him on my desk, and especially now, I stop to say, "Thanks, Babar" for his message.

Babar is a survivor. In the first few pages of his story we witness the murder of his mother. It is cruel and sad. But Babar moves from the country to the city where he meets the Old Lady who becomes his mentor. With her guidance he learns to dress well—he's French after all—in green suit and spats, and he acquires the skill of conversation in the Paris salons. But most importantly Babar moves beyond simply surviving to use his past to become an individual with deep values and strong character.

Eventually, with changing times and the call of the needy, Babar turns to social responsibility and goes home to help the citizens of his country.

Babar is a model leader. He marries Celeste and has a family. His country prospers and there is balance and respect in Celesteville a community rich with diversity. The only really bad time comes when Celesteville is burned and Babar has the bad dream. In his dream demons come—hairy winged things named hate, fear, greed. But Babar summons the spirits of patience and hope and chases the demons out of the country and peace is restored.

Babar is completely comfortable with himself; that's what recommends him the most. Though he is certain of his authority, and wears a crown to prove it, he is neither heavy handed nor a workaholic. Babar seems to have the faith to really live one day at a time. (Did he go to therapy? Elephants Anonymous? de Brunhoff doesn't say.)

Babar inspires. He is profoundly honest, he negotiates change, he's committed to family and country and he sends this overriding message: "Don't panic." Babar is a model for how to express one's individuality through, not in spite of, self-control. (How very French, non?) He gives us hope that a wise and caring leader is possible, one who advocates for peace but who is also not afraid to go after demons if they threaten his people.

Babar could be just the leader we need now. Wouldn't you love to see him at the UN? He could bridge East and West, or even France and the rest of the world. Babar reaches across culture, language and even strategic alliances to teach peace.

Just to imagine the spirit and heart of the woman who created the world's favorite elephant makes me smile. When we see the American and Iraqi families who are grieving now, is it a surprise that someone's mother created a leader like Babar?

Au revoir, Cécile, and Thank you.

Thanksgiving: Grateful for Mixed Blessings

On Thursday many of us will be sitting down to dinner with family or friends and gratitude will be mentioned as we offer a blessing on the meal. It's appropriate to the day of course; we know the Pilgrim's story of thankfulness for surviving their first difficult year in the New World.

At many of our tables there will be a nod to the formerly religious aspect of the day. Someone will suggest, "Let's go around the table and everyone say what they're grateful for."

It's easy at times like this to name good health, career success, and our kid's accomplishments, but we often forget that some of our best gifts don't come in pretty wrapping. I suggest that we put a new spin on this tradition. This year ask your guests: What are the mixed blessings in your life this year?

Here are some examples: There was the day you were running late and therefore missed the big accident or traffic jam; or the day you skipped church but when channel surfing heard a speaker or story that gave you a new outlook on life; Maybe it was the day you got lost in a new part of town but in your wandering found a store that sold exactly what you had been hunting for months. Get the idea?

Then try upping the ante a bit: How about when you got fired but at out-placement you found the work you really want to do? Maybe the person you wanted to marry said "No" and broke your heart, but months later you met the one you were supposed to make a life with.

You get the idea, but let's push it a bit farther. How about the serious illness that knocked you off your feet, but having to stay in bed gave you time to recast your life? Or maybe the struggle to accept a more permanent disability made it plain who your friends are or revealed a talent you didn't know you had?

Okay, even harder now: What about the death of a loved one that devastated you, but one day in the midst of grief you felt something other than pain and realized you were feeling joy like nothing you had ever felt, and you knew that you were able to feel it because the grief had cracked you open. Similarly, we get a gift from someone else's death when we see just how very short life is and decide to quit with the worry/status/fear already and go live our lives.

These mixed blessings are not easy to accept or admit, and sometimes it is just faith itself that is the gift. It can be in the midst of terrible things that we're forced to develop trust, and then we find, when the crisis is over, that we have a new belief.

Of course the graduate school level of this kind of gratitude is saying, "Thank you" even before the good part comes. If you've had experience with mixed blessings, you begin to know-- even while life is painful or unpleasant-- that there will be meaning in it. And so we say Thank you –purely on faith –even when we're getting hit hard.

Yes, some of these blessings come in less than Hallmark moments. Maybe it was feedback from a friend that clued you in on the truth about some personality flaws, or the DWI that was humiliating and expensive was also what made you take a look at your problem and change your life. Maybe it was an emotional breakdown that allowed you to put yourself back together in a new and stronger way.

As parents we coach our kids with, "What do you say?" for gifts, or favors or compliments given. Can we learn to say that to ourselves when life hands us a package that isn't very pretty?

So when that "What are you grateful for?" comes around at your Thanksgiving table this year don't groan, but dig deep. Name the blessings that came from pain and grief and loss and trouble. When we can say, Thanks for both the good and the bad, for easy and hard times, then, just like the Pilgrims, we'll have a real Thanksgiving.

Grocery Carts and Community

It began as a joke. Each time we went grocery shopping I was annoyed to find shopping carts all over the lot and blocking so many parking spaces. I started to refer to them as "abandoned" and joked about "rescuing" them. I'd always returned my own cart because it was fun; it was a leftover from childhood when taking the cart back was a treat. My brothers and I always fought to see who'd get to ride the cart—like a scooter-- back to the store's curb.

Over time, I began to notice how many people were not willing to walk even the few steps to the "corral," that chute in the middle of the lot to place their cart out of harm's way. Now, this may offend some, but it needs to be asked: What kind of person leaves a grocery cart in the middle of the parking lot? Is it about trying to save time?

I do know how busy we all are, so I went to the store parking lot one day and I timed it. From every part of the lot-- from the "good" parking spaces to the ones in the outfield-- it never took me more than 45 seconds to get the cart back to the curb. The average consumer makes 94 supermarket trips each year—so that's less than two minutes out of your week.

OK, I know that if you have an infant and a toddler and two bags of groceries, maybe you can't take the cart back. But some of us who don't have our hands quite that full could offer to help. That would be a truly radical act. But generally, as I've learned in my cart-stalking mode, it's not the parents who are skipping the cart return. It's the rest of us who could handle it just fine.

One day as I was loading my groceries into my car, a woman arriving to shop asked, "Want me to take that cart back for you?" That day I got it. Her gesture was more than an act of kindness; it was an act of community.

I know that a cart is just a cart, but shopping carts are also a critical—and consuming--symbol of our culture. What we do with our shopping cart is symptomatic of how we participate in society. The grocery store, perhaps even more than the church, is the place we ultimately come to for sustenance. We say we want more real neighborhoods. Well, returning the cart is a tiny measure of our true intentions. When we don't take the cart back, we are leaving the creation of our community to someone else.

There are added benefits in this simple act. Who isn't talking about getting more exercise? So walk the cart back for selfish reasons. Or consider it a form of meditation. In the brief span of time it takes to roll the cart you can reflect on what it means to be in partnership with other human beings.

There is no bargain way of life, no coupons to get a free taste of community. In this time of speeches and sound bites about democracy it's the small things that make us true citizens. Community is created in simple daily acts: Saying good morning, tossing the neighbor's paper closer to their door, and picking up litter—yeah, someone else's--and returning the grocery cart, are tiny ways of taking responsibility. That one gesture contains it all: connection, responsibility, participation.

Faith grows from willingness the size of a mustard seed, and character can grow from a tiny act like returning a shopping cart: Sixty seconds to citizenship.

It's not somebody else's community. It's ours. We create it and claim it and enjoy its privileges one lonely cart at a time.

Happy Introvert Day

Ahhh, January 2. The day that introverts get to breathe a sigh of relief. We can come out of hiding; it's safe to answer the phone, and to stop pretending we feel the flu coming on. Hip Hip Hooray! The holidays are over.

Yes, from mid-December through New Year's Day, those of us with an introverted nature live in a state of perpetual dread. The weeks of office parties, neighborhood potlucks and open houses drain all our energy. But today we can relax; we made it through.

I speak from experience. My name is Diane and I am an introvert. It surprises most people because I'm outgoing and friendly and, in fact, very far from shy, but I prefer one person and one conversation at a time.

I fought this for years, always trying to be someone else. I made myself go to parties; I tried to fix what I thought was "wrong" with me. It didn't help that other people would press, "But you're so good with people," as if being introverted meant living on the dark side. But I finally got it.

This is also one of the blessings of being older. Along with the wrinkles comes a "What you see is what you get" self-acceptance, or perhaps for introverts it's, "Who you don't see is what you get." It is a great relief to stop trying to be who you're not.

But it's no wonder that we introverts are sometimes defensive. Seventy-five percent of the population is extroverted; we're outnumbered three-to-one, and the American culture tends to reward extroversion, while being disdainful and suspicious of reflection and solitude.

I've learned to spot us though. We're the folks walking toward a festive house saying, "How long do we have to stay?" Or we're the ones in the center of the room assessing other's interactions, and slowly backing toward the door. Introverts crave meaning, so party chitchat feels like sandpaper to our psyche.

Here's what introverts are not: We're not afraid and we're not shy. Introversion has little to do with fear or reticence. We're just focused, and we prefer one-on-one because we like to listen and we want to follow an idea all the way through to another interesting idea. Consequently small talk annoys us. So does pretending to be happy or excited or anything that we're not.

Many great leaders are introverts and I think that many of our better presidents have been introverts: Lincoln, Carter and the John Adams—both father and son. No, maybe I'm not being totally fair, but life isn't fair to introverts. Introverted kids are pressured to "speak up" and "make friends" or told they're not leaders. We're hounded to "be more outgoing" and tortured with invitations that begin, "Why don't we all…" No thanks, we don't want to do anything that involves "we" and "all"; we prefer to visit you, just you, and not a dozen other people.

The philosopher Pascal wrote, "The sole cause of man's unhappiness is that he does not know how to stay quietly in his room." Introverts do.

So let's make January 2ⁿᵈ Happy Introvert Day. We'll be quiet and happy. As a bonus, January's weather is on our side.

You say it might snow? Oh darn, I guess I'll have to stay home.

The Easter Brother

I consider the following to be quite telling about my own personality: I never believed in Santa Claus. I never, even as a little kid, imagined or believed that a man would go house to house in a red suit and bring toys and stockings to boys and girls.

I did, however, believe, until I was ten or maybe even older, in the Easter Bunny. In my own defense I have to explain that we lived near the woods and I saw all kinds of rabbits, little baby bunnies and distance-covering jack rabbits, all the time. But I also had two older brothers who, as only big brothers can, facilitated, my belief. Sig and Larry would talk just slightly out of my earshot about The Bunny. "Don't let her see him," and "Did you see the basket he left next door?" They also, to make it more convincing, put bite marks on the handles of our Easter baskets.

My brothers died when they were 42 and 48. Now I'm the oldest. At Easter I miss them. I miss having an Easter basket from Lar who –even as an adult—made me one that included the bunny's teeth marks to remind me just how naïve I had been. And I miss our sibling tradition of finding the family "King Egg." As Easter approached we would each decorate our own hard-boiled egg, fortifying them with dye and crayon and competed (Sig and Lar both went on to become engineers) by ramming our colored eggs together to see whose broke first.

I also miss dressing up for Easter services, complete with new dress and corsage. The three of us continued to go to church on Easter even when we had walked away from organized religion. We kept this holiday because we all liked the uplifting Easter hymns like "Up From the Grave He Arose.".

I kept going to church on Easter even as, and after, Sig and Larry were dying, because those Easter hymns gave me a weird hope. It was not a hope of miraculous recovery for either brother, or necessarily for a reunion in the "Great Beyond," but hope for my own "arose" from the heartache of losing my brothers, my playmates, co-conspirators and occasional torturers.

One of my final conversations with Sig was about my car. I was 40 years old but still easily defeated by my car worries. Larry, who was then sick, was caring for Sig, who was dying, and I called their house in tears to report the impending death of my car. Larry, who was on the phone with me, relayed the mechanic's opinion to Sig who was lying in what would soon be his deathbed.

Lar said to me, "Sig wants to talk to you." I was surprised because Sig's speech had become painful and very difficult for him. I waited until Larry positioned the phone for Sig to talk. "Here's what you tell them….," he began, and he proceeded to dictate a set of car repair instructions to convince any mechanic that I knew a nut from a bolt, and that this girl had a brother who would not see his sister taken for a ride.

At Easter I have the best memories of a girl with brothers—of a basket-carrying rabbit who was "just here a second ago" and of making faces to spoil the, "Come on; say cheese" Brownie snapshots that Dad took of our Easter outfits.

Apart from any theology, Easter lets me believe in the resurrection of my family, of my all too gullible girlhood self, and in a life that rises, falls, rises and dies over and over as we each cycle through layers of loss and gain.

April is Poetry Month

April is National Poetry Month. This means poets on postage stamps; poem-a-day emails and poets-in-the-schools are working overtime. But if talking about poetry makes you shudder, you're not alone.

For many people the thought of poetry brings back memories of seventh grade. If we were lucky we had an English teacher who loved poetry so much that when he or she read poems aloud, we could viscerally experience the power of words meeting air.

But there were other teachers who made us memorize Old English or deconstruct poems about marriage and mortality, topics not exactly top-of-mind for 12-year-olds. The bad 7th grade poetry scenario went like this: The teacher read a poem that described a rose opening on a summer day, and we thought, "Oh, the poem must be about summer, or beauty or nature, right?" But the teacher would sigh heavily and say, "No, this poem is speaking about war and man's inhumanity to man." After repetitions of that experience many people never wanted to pick up a book of poetry again. We'd come away feeling that the deck was stacked in this "what does the poem mean" business, and that poems were a code we couldn't crack.

This month we get another chance. We have April in which to reclaim poetry— good, bad or even silly—as part of our lives. After all, before 7th grade teachers got hold of it, poetry was our first language, our history, and even our music. We don't have to let it drift away. It's our right to take poetry back and to remember that poetry is in the Psalms, in nursery rhymes, and at the heart of many children's stories. After all, "Green Eggs and Ham" is a poem too.

Part of reclaiming poetry, though, is recognizing poets. We don't have poet celebrities in the United States as some other countries do. In Canada poet Ann Carson is on magazine covers and they write about what she wears and where she goes. In Chile Pablo Neruda was a diplomat. We do have a Poet Laureate of the United States but when most people hear of Billy Collins, they think he's a ballplayer. One of our finest poets, Robert Bly, didn't register in American consciousness until, after 40 years and 20 books of poetry, he wrote a self-help book for men.

We have tiny bits of poetry in our civic life. Bill Clinton gave Maya Angelou recognition when he asked her to read at his inauguration. But she was only the second poet ever to read at a presidential swearing in. Robert Frost had been first, reciting "The Gift Outright" at John Kennedy's ceremony in 1961.

That's a reminder that there are poems that belong to certain times and events. Kennedy's Inaugural is an example. Because of the sun's glare that January morning Robert Frost could not read the poem he had written for that day, so he recited his older poem, "The Gift Outright," with its famous lines: "Something we were withholding made us weak/ Until we found it was ourselves we were withholding from our land of living/...Such as we were we gave ourselves outright."

Later that "filler" poem had perfect resonance for our "Ask not what your country..." president.

Sometimes poems come out of an event and at other times an older poem helps us make sense of the present.

Auden's "September 1, 1939," passed around and read aloud after September 11th [was] the perfect poem for our own sad autumn.

William Carlos Williams said it in one of his poems:

It is difficult
to get the news from poems.
Yet men die miserably every day,
for lack
of what is found there.

Maybe what the 7th grade teacher knew back then that we didn't was that poems can help and they can heal and sometimes they can communicate what no treatise or speech ever will.

A Day Without Cameras

A few weeks ago I visited the Metropolitan Museum of Art. While going through the galleries I noticed something that first annoyed and then worried me. I found it was difficult to get a good view of the paintings because other visitors kept walking in front of me. At first I thought, "This must be a cultural difference" assuming they were foreign visitors, but when I stepped back to see what was going on, I realized that while some were foreign tourists many were Americans. Watching them, I realized that they didn't notice that they were walking in front of people because they were always looking through their cameras.

As I watched this strange behavior, I realized that the camera-clad folks were not pushing to get a better look at the artwork—most of them did not look directly at the paintings or sculpture at all. In most cases they would walk up to a work of art, look through the camera, select their shot, click and move on. Some never saw the art directly; rather they used the camera to document what they saw, or more accurately, what they never saw.

What was most worrisome was that in addition to capturing proof of having not seen great art, the camera-tourists were oblivious to the other visitors around them. Looking through their cameras they were able to stay apart from the art and also from their fellow human beings.

Here is the sad aesthetic irony: Works of art are made by human beings for other human beings. An artist works to communicate the deepest connection –perspectives and ideas-- with other people.

Great artists give deeply of themselves in creating their work. It seems that the least they can ask of us, who freely come to museums, is that we stop and look, repaying them with our attention.

In a museum like The Metropolitan, where some of the greatest art is collected, we can assume that these works offer us some of the best reminders of our universal connections to other people, near and far, in both geography and time.

That is why the best museums attract us—we want to see what was created by artists and what they have to tell us. But maybe now, cameras raised in front, we prefer not to see but to have seen.

I left the museum making a wish for: A Day without Cameras. I invite you to try it. One vacation day with no camera. No digital, no video and no cell. If you are camera dependent –as The Met visitors seemed to be--you may not remember that the human eye, using extraordinary technology called the retina and the brain, also records images.

Cameras are wonderful but they fool us into thinking we can "take" a picture, but we can't really. We're tempted to believe that we can capture an experience that is intended for here and now, in the moment. Yes, we all have that desire for a souvenir or a reminder. But most museums and beautiful sites have anticipated that need. They have arranged for the best photographer to take the best picture from the best angle with the best camera. You can take home that postcard for less than a dollar.

Art has power to ignite our imagination, to stimulate our thinking and to provide enjoyment, but for that to happen there is an unspoken rule—kind of like you have at a casino: You must be present to win.

So for one day lower your camera. There's no telling what you might see.

Aging and Shoes

Last week, browsing in a Toronto shoe store, I began eavesdropping on a mother and daughter shopping for shoes. The conversation brought back memories: "I don't care what you like; we're not buying those, try on the other pair." The customer stares straight ahead. More exasperation, "For the party you can get what you like, but we're not buying those". One is rolling her eyes at the shoe salesman; the other slouches in her seat. I remember scenes like this from my teen years, but now it is the 50-something daughter doing the chastising and the 80-something mother annoyed and humiliated that she can't buy the shoes she likes. I can see pain on the daughter's face as she explains, "The doctor said you can't wear slip-ons; you have to have tie shoes because of your cane."

We can track the progression of women's lives through shoe shopping. Little girls can't wait to give up babyish tie shoes for big-girl loafers, then out of loafers and into heels, then wanting cool sneakers, and back and forth, until a grown daughter is telling her mother that she can't buy slip-on shoes any more.

On the surface taking our mother shoe shopping is not new, but to be the one holding the credit card and saying yea or nay to clothing, menu and housing selections puts adult children in places we never expected to travel to emotionally.

It happens that I am in this store on this day because I am waiting while my husband meets with his mother's banker. For many years—as a precaution in case of emergency—he's had her power of attorney. We always imagined the emergency would be an accident or catastrophic illness, but this day we are in town because this crisis rose slowly. Mom's accounts are confusing her and she can't keep track of bills, so today her grown son is taking away her credit cards just as he took the car keys a few years ago.

We are comforted intellectually by knowing that this is the "right thing to do," but emotionally no one prepares us to parent our own parent.

As each generation lives longer we are finding ourselves in the middle and doing double duty; we're the "Sandwich Generation" with kids of our own and parents whose needs mirror those of kids.

An estimated 22 million US households are caring for a relative over 50, and when I compare notes with friends, we realize we cover the same topics with our kids and our parents. We talk about drugs and alcohol, driving, handling money and credit wisely, and yes, even sex.

In a bookstore I browse in the Parenting section and transpose the titles to get at this role reversal. There is the "What to Expect" series for new moms, and "Talking So Your Teen Will Listen" but where is "What to expect as your parents age," and "How to talk so your 86- year-old mother will listen"?

At parenting workshops we role-play and rehearse scripts to help us be "assertive-yet-loving" and to "set clear boundaries." We're advised to send a clear message about who is the adult. Well, who is the adult in the world of aging parents?

We let our kids blow their money to experience the natural consequence of their choices. Should we allow our parents to do the same?

Perhaps the best we can do is to take advantage of the fact that our own future caretakers are standing right beside us when we tell Gramma that she can't drive or buy the shoes she likes. We need to tell our own kids, "Someday this will be you and me, and I am now giving you permission when that day comes to take away my car keys and my slippery shoes--and to remind me how painful this was."

We may be wearing our own slip-on shoes for a few more years, but, in fact, we need to walk in the moccasins of both our parents and our kids as we negotiate this narrow passage in our mid- life.

Commencement Speeches

It is the season of commencement speeches. High schools and colleges near and far are celebrating their graduates by hosting celebrity speechmakers. We listen for sound bites from the Bills—Clinton, Cosby and Gates-- along with CEOs and novelists, college presidents and politicians. Most of their talks inspire, but there has come to be an underlying message linking education, graduation and material success. There is an implied link between tuition and expected future wages that seems to suggest that's the transaction in full. But in our excitement for the graduates, are we putting the emphasis in the wrong place?

It is true that for many people education is an inoculation against poverty, the guarantee of a good job and a boost up the ladder of success. But as we look around the world, we are reminded that what that ladder leans against is equally important.

Our Founding Fathers knew that an educated citizenry was the only means of preserving a true democracy. We get confused sometimes thinking that the core of our democratic process is about how many groups are represented or assuring majority rule, but in fact we've misunderstood the true engine of democracy.

Democracy is not about "the majority," rather it's about debate. Invented by the rational Greeks, democracy is about arguing freely in order to arrive at the wisest and most sensible conclusion for a community or a country. "Majority rule" is merely the means of deciding the outcome of the debate. Full debate—not just sound bites--requires critical thinking, hence the crucial role of education.

The commencement speeches will include platitudes about how lucky we are to be Americans. And we are. But our freedom is not guaranteed. Living in a democracy is not a right that comes gift-wrapped just for being born at this geographic address. Debate is the minimum fee to purchase citizenship, and freedom of speech goes hand-in-hand with true and open debate. This matters right now as we are enjoying a longer period of debate in this year's pre-election process.

Thomas Jefferson, who wrote our famous Declaration, knew that to preserve the form of government he was creating, America would require educated, thoughtful and discerning citizens. Education mattered to him and the others so much because they understood that education would be the constant and stable ground under the new government, not an escalator to lift Americans to big jobs and high-status salaries.

Jefferson and the other founders valued education not so that the United States would someday lead the world's economy, but to ensure longevity for the form of government they were birthing. It was central to their vision of future generations enjoying a genuine constitutional democracy. Jefferson wrote: "If a nation expects it can be ignorant and free, in a state of civilization, it expects what never was and never can be."

It's easy in our pressured lives to forget how fragile our democracy is. We're too busy to watch the news, to vote, to write our leaders. But this very good life that keeps us too busy to be good citizens is at risk.

This year, especially with war, an election and the economic crisis before us we get to see why education is crucial to maintaining a truly democratic form of government.

Education can and should empower citizens to participate. If a diploma can help one to get a better job or to make more money, that's a bonus. At the heart of mastering reading, writing and rhetoric is the winning ticket that ensures a genuinely democratic way of life.

Random Acts of Feminism

It's estimated that between 500,000 and one million people attended the Women's Rights rally in Washington, DC. Women and men traveled from all over the US and many more wished they could go. Some of us who stayed home wondered if we missed a chance to express our feminist convictions. We must remember that while public acts are important, there are also equally valuable and sometimes more powerful random acts of feminism.

A random act of feminism is that seemingly small and spontaneous gesture that offers support for women. Here are some of the daily ways we can all rally for women: Be present to women who are struggling, especially younger women. They don't need to be fixed or rescued, but a well placed, "Good for you" and sincere admiration goes a long way. Be someone that young people feel safe talking to about the difficult things they face. If feminism is about creating richer, more complex models of womanhood with more choices, then support options for the many choices women have to make for work, health and family. Share honestly the good and bad of your choices. Mentor someone. Respect different tactics in the service of shared goals.

One simple but critical act of feminism each of us can perform is letting those around us know that we have zero tolerance for family violence. It isn't hard. You need only be the broken record that says firmly, "That's not OK," anytime you hear of a woman being hit or bullied. Our daughters need to hear it and so do our sons as well as friends, coworkers and sometimes even strangers.

A must-do act of feminism is getting women to vote. Ask every woman you know, from now until October, "Are you registered?" Pick up some extra forms at the post office and hand them out.

We can also commit acts of feminism with our wallets, not just by contributing to women's organizations, but also by making sure we spend our money to ensure better lives for women. Ask the businesses you deal with if they are women owned, if women are part of management and if they are family friendly. Tell them that it matters in your purchasing decisions, whether the item costs five bucks or $5,000. You might consider what a friend of mine did when she was about to purchase a new luxury car: Call ahead and ask if there is a female sales associate. Support organizations that give women opportunities.

Some acts of feminism fall into the "Don't" category: Don't compare your feminism to that of younger women. Don't say, "When I was her age..." We never were their age in this age. It doesn't compare. Don't squint or turn away when you hear about injustice or violence against women. Sometimes, for very good reasons, we can't intervene in the moment, but don't confuse being able to solve a problem with admitting that there is one. It's never right to pretend an injustice hasn't occurred just because we can't fix it. And don't gossip; not gossiping about other women is a powerful act of feminism.

There are lots of ways to be an activist. Most don't require wearing buttons or carrying signs. Last year Gloria Steinem offered this advice: "Think of the worst thing that ever happened to you, and how you survived that, and use those methods politically."

Margaret Mead taught us, "Never doubt that a small group of thoughtful, committed citizens can change the world. Indeed, it is the only thing that ever has." Yes, and sometimes it can be a very, very small group: just two people. And sometimes it can be just you saying: Yes or No or Stop.

Good and Evil in All of Us

We don't talk much about evil these days. We find it almost embarrassing to use the word. We reserve discussions of good and evil for church, and even there, we cringe if a minister spends too much time on evil.

But lately there have been stories in our news –shootings, stabbings, beatings, murders. When we hear about kids who kill and people who kill kids, our curiosity is more than morbid.

"How do things like that happen?" We're enamored of TV shows like CSI, but even as solving crime becomes more "scientific", we're not satisfied. That's because we ask the wrong question. We're not really interested in "Who done it?" What haunts us is why. Why do people kill?

With all of our forensic science we are missing a piece that our ancestors had. They struggled less because they found an explanation in the existence of evil.

Colonial America had its share of killing: child-child murders, mother-child murders and spousal killing. Nothing modern about that. But what was unique was how the community explained those acts to itself. Historian Karen Halttunen writes about this in her book Murder Most Foul.

Public executions in the 18th century included a sermon. No separation of church and state. The execution sermon was a talk about sin and redemption. The murderer was not treated as a monster but as a fallen member of the community. The evil in the killer was not presumed to be anything other than that existing in everyone, all sharing original sin.

By the 19th century God and Satan began to recede in our social consciousness. Our separation doctrines were enabled by that shift. But it meant that evil acts couldn't be explained the same way. But we still need explanations so murderers had to become outsiders, aliens and monsters.

That's one of the reasons that stories and movies about killers are so popular. It's our 18th century petticoat showing. Murder demands that a community come to terms with a crime, so we keep trying to put terrible acts in context. Some part of us wants to believe in evil and wants reassurance that it's not in us.

So, like our forebears we look to anointed persons to help us make sense of murder. But instead of ministers we turn to secular experts. Our contemporary execution sermons come from our cultural "clergy": trial analysts, defense attorneys, memoir writers and, of course, talk show hosts.

We want explanation and reassurance, so our experts point to poverty, broken families, violent games, even chemicals in our food. We shrink from what our elders grasped. We are looking for something outside us so we don't have to consider what might be in us.

Renowned psychoanalyst Thomas Szasz brings us back when he talks about what most upsets a community when there is a murder.

"We say that killing is "unimaginable" but that's not true; murder is among the most imaginable crimes," Szasz explains. While most people cannot imagine killing a stranger, they have at some time felt enough rage to kill an in-law, spouse, child or sibling.

"That is why," Szasz says, "we have the stories of Abraham and Isaac, and Cain and Abel." Humans create social taboos to stabilize a community and that is why, says Szasz, we are deeply unsettled when someone commits murder. What the 18th century satisfied with theology we answer with psychology. The answer lies somewhere in-between and somewhere in us. The biggest murder mystery is that we don't really know why people kill --or if we could.

Barbie at 40

I have always thought that one of the best feelings in the world comes from being able to help someone who has befriended me. As 1999 approaches it occurs to me that an old friend of mine is about to turn 40. Now I get the chance to show her the lay of this mid-life land.

I was just five years old when Barbie was born and I wanted a life just like hers. Barbie had a boyfriend, Ken; a best friend Midge; and a lot of clothes. From Barbie I learned a sartorial approach to life. One need only have the right outfit and the life to go with it would appear: Buy a poofy dress and then get a date for the prom; plan a trousseau and marriage would follow; buy the right suit and a career would materialize. Now, suddenly, I'm 45 and Barbie is about to turn 40. We're both older and wiser, but some of Barbie's lessons need revising.

Do you remember how Barbie's life came packaged so neatly with each outfit in a clear plastic bubble and each part carefully labeled for the occasion? There was "Barbie's Sock Hop" with a poodle skirt, tight sweater, and tiny 45rpm records. Other outfits were for going to the movies, horseback riding and even a "Study Date At The Library."

But Barbie has evolved--we all do by 40--and Mattel has tried to keep her up to date. But I'm wondering: Has Mattel really prepared Barbie for her 40's? Most women my age know that a closet full of cute outfits is not enough for this time of life. Here are some of the things I want to tell my old friend about what she'll need for this next phase of life.

The first thing I'd recommend is a new best friend. In the 1960's Midge was the perfect best friend for a pretty girl: friendly, loyal and slightly less attractive. Barbie, in your forties you'll need friends who have shoulders you can cry on and who are smarter than you about work and relationships and life. One of the fun things about 40 plus friends is that you get to pass the wisdom back and forth. Your friends tell you today what you told them last week, and next month you send the same words back in their direction. At 40 you cry for each other and pray for each other and show up when the bad stuff happens.

This leads to another necessity for Barbie's new life. If Mattel ever found a way to package this, it would be a best seller. They might call it "Barbie's 12 Step Program" but which one? Looking at Barbie's closets she might have a bit of a compulsive shopping problem or maybe Overeaters Anonymous would be her group. This is the program for anorexics, bulimics, anyone with a food problem. You have to wonder how she's kept that unnatural figure all these years. I've never seen Barbie drink so she doesn't need AA, but the 12 steps can't hurt anyone, and besides, every woman over 40 needs some kind of support group.

Of course after dates and dating, Barbie's focus was always her career. She was a nurse, doctor, lawyer, even astronaut, but that's not so bad. She's kind of like most women I know in their 40's. We're all still trying to decide what we want to be when we grow up. But I would have to tell Barbie that there is another kind of work coming her way in these forty-something years. While our jobs may not be as settled as we imagined at 25 or 30, in our 40's we begin to find what writer Laurie Colwin called "our population." By that Colwin meant the people in the world that we are meant to help. For Colwin, who was a food writer and novelist, her "population" turned out to be homeless women who were mentally ill. One day a week Colwin cooked for them. This kind of community service is not the busy, busy volunteer variety of earlier days. It's not about meeting people or adding to your resume. And Barb, you won't need any new outfits for this part. It's not an event, there's no "Barbie's Night At The Shelter." Doing service is just part of your life.

What else would I want to tell this old friend as I toast her upcoming 40th? I'd have to thank her for her fashion advice, but I'd add my own now. When I was little Barbie taught me about matching shoes to purses. But I've learned a few things about putting yourself together after 40. Barb, the really good stuff is not in your closet. At my age it's the losses and heartbreaks and the mistakes that make you an original. I'm not talking about pretty, pastel faux pas here; I mean horrid, messy, head-shaking mistakes. Those, when worn with a little self-forgiveness and a lot of gratitude, are what become the really fine accessories for a woman of her 40's.

Mattel is on the right track. Barbie has arms and legs that flex now and she can turn her head to look behind her. And at 40 Barbie has knees that bend now so she can pray. And that's a good thing. It isn't easy being plastic.

A Closer Look at the Easter Bunny

One of my favorite Easter stories comes from a friend whose toddler was attending a progressive nursery school. Because the school was fiercely non-denominational, they were careful about celebrating holidays but got caught, as schools do, wanting to acknowledge various events without emphasizing the religious origins. So the school told parents that they would have a visit from the "Spring Rabbit."

On the day of the celebration my friend told her little boy, "Today the Spring Rabbit is coming to your school." Her son burst into tears and said, "No, Mama, I don't want the Spring Rabbit, I want the Easter Bunny." He knew. The Easter Bunny matters.

This week I have been sighing. I sigh when I hear the rants on TV and read the misguided articles about how the Easter Bunny is one more example of the commercial exploitation of Christianity. It's a reprise of the Santa Claus/Christmas rant.

This accusation that the Easter Bunny takes something away from Easter ignores the fact that the creators of Easter did more than a teensy bit of taking from previous holidays. The celebration of spring, of light returning from darkness, is ancient. It was part of Celtic and Mesopotamian cultures. The Bunny—well, back then he was a rabbit—was part of Phoenician festivals as early as 1100 BC. Because rabbits are energetic and prolific, they were considered expressive of the power of life to wake from death in the spring.

While our Christian Easter celebrates Christ rising from the dead, it is named after the Goddess of dawn, Eastre and her celebration of the rebirth of the sun this time of year.

Can it hurt to acknowledge previous contributors to our culture? Surely our beliefs are big enough and our faith deep enough to not fear what came before. Ours is a culture of assimilation and our holidays are mostly overlays of ancient religions. That's not a bad thing, just a history thing.

It is so easy to "tut-tut," or perhaps "cluck", about the Easter Bunny and toss off accusations like "exploiting the sacred," but that's just lazy thinking. There's more to this rabbit or he wouldn't have stuck around all this time. As a Christian I think we have to give the Easter Bunny his due.

So what's this Bunny about? He is, of course, about fertility, and a fairly voracious strain: He's a male rabbit who lays eggs in a nest, carries them in a basket, and then hides them for children to find. It's quite a picture when you think about it.

But there's something even more important for us to consider about the Easter Bunny. The Easter Bunny brings gifts for children but, unlike Santa Claus, who comes into our home and brings gifts to the safety of our hearth, the Easter Bunny calls us to come outdoors to look for his eggs. The Easter Bunny invites us to come into the world.

There is a very old belief that on Easter morning the sun dances. If, as we say, heaven is on earth, then it makes sense that we have to step out of our homes or our work-- whatever we bury ourselves in--to experience it. And we do that with others who are also coming out to look around.

The poet Kathleen Norris offers this from her research: According to recent scriptural scholarship Jesus's saying, "The Kingdom of God is within you," should be more accurately rendered as "The kingdom of God is among you." So with apologies to ministers who are struggling for just the right words for Sunday's sermon, Easter is less about who is in the pulpit and more about who is in the pews.

We go inside to find one kind of spirituality, but ultimately we have to roll away our own stones and come into the world. The Bunny calls us outward to join our fellows and to look around our lives.

Hippity-hoppity Easter's on its way.

The Language Police

Years ago I worked for a company that was very committed to diversity. We had programs and guidelines and trainings and it was great. But after a while, in our enthusiasm for inclusion, we went from celebrating differences to pretending there were none. In the name of diversity we banned religious symbols and bumper stickers and even Halloween costumes. We pretended we didn't notice race, gender or disability. One day I knew we had gone over the good-intentions edge when I heard a manager tell a visitor, "We have many diverse people here."

That comes back to me now because I've been reading about The Language Police, a new book by historian Diane Ravitch. She's published a glossary of words and images that are banned by editors of education and government publications. Certainly you can guess at some of the words, the ones that most of us have learned not to say.

But Ravitch has found that those are just the tip of the good intentions iceberg. Among the examples in the glossary are duffer and egghead. Well, OK. But also banned is the elderly, which is to be replaced by the term "older people." Now, a good editor might ask "older than whom?" Elderly has some specificity. Older is relative.

But more than bad writing is at stake. The list also bans the word fairy. Fairy is not permitted, according to Ravitch, because it suggests homosexuality. The educator's recommendation? "Replace with elf."

Now anyone who reads children's lit, or loves art or favors alternative gardening knows that there is a world of difference between a fairy and an elf. If the issue is one of education, wouldn't a better response to youngsters who tee-hee at fairy be to talk about why that word came to have those overtones? You'd get a history lesson and a diversity discussion. Certainly shushing the word fairy sends a clear message that there is something wrong with fairies, garden variety or other.

But the glossary goes further in limiting what young people and the citizenry should see and say. Also banned is the word hut. The guidelines suggest that hut is ethnocentric and should be replaced with "small house." Now it seems to me that this switch-a-roo comes dangerously close to teaching that life in poor countries isn't so bad; Third World people just have little houses instead of big ones.

Ravitch's outing of these banned words might be something to laugh at if it were not so scary. It's frightening to learn that our textbooks and publications –our language –is changed this way. No, we don't want to see African Americans shown as baggage handlers—also on the banned list-- and we don't want to characterize the older persons as "senile"—also banned. But when Pollyanna is sexist and yacht is elitist ("use big boat") then we have lost our sense along with our sensibility. We risk being as well as sounding vacuous.

Words are not just dots of ink or puffs of air. They are the raw material of thought, which is what we use to shape our ideas and beliefs. We need all kinds of words-- even troubling ones—with which to think broadly and deeply. Not having words for terrible or difficult things doesn't make them go away; in fact it makes it even easier for them to sneak up on us.

We want our words back. This craving shows up in popular culture. The popularity of shows like the Osbornes and Simpsons and South Park are the backlash and the shadow side of political correctness and the language police.

Being on the brink of war, we need to pay attention to what happens to our words: thought control, propaganda and ideology are built with them. We'll have little thought life and fewer choices if we do not claim our differences and defend the meaning of our words.

Abuse Survivors: The Other Olympians

The Olympics have begun. Most of us love the Olympics because we admire the hard work and endurance of elite athletes from around the world. In Olympic stories we hear the narrative of intense commitment, working through pain, triumph over adversity, and the ability to return again and again after injury and through hardship.

There is another group of people who are so much like Olympic athletes, who have all of those qualities, but who are mostly invisible. I've been thinking about them this week because of the other big sports story in our news—the tragedy and crime at Penn State. That other extraordinary group is the adults who survive childhood abuse.

I know something about this because I am one of them. I am a survivor of childhood physical and sexual abuse. I know the emotional, physical, psychic and economic cost of surviving to adulthood with a decent and competent life.

When I was 10 years old our family doctor gave my mother a prescription for Dexedrine and she was quickly hooked. My mother's addiction left her with violent mood swings and tragically blind to family members and neighbors who were dangerous. It was an eight-year nightmare.

Some of the abuse I tried to tell family members about and some I told no one. The personal cost was very high. I spent years drowning in self-doubt, shame and anxiety, becoming dangerously anorexic and, of course, succumbing to my own addictions. Finally at age 28, in excruciating physical and emotional pain, I got help.

My recovery from abuse was it's own terrifying roller-coaster ride. The only thing harder than living through abuse in childhood is the endurance of re-experiencing it as an adult in therapy. Years of therapy. Expensive therapy. Over the last 30 years I've helped to buy some beautiful homes and at least one sailboat in treatment fees paid out of pocket. I don't regret a dime of it. But I do think about the others like the boys and men at Penn State. Who will help them?

We've heard that the penalty for Penn State will include funds for prevention of child abuse, but where are the millions for the decades-long treatment needed by Penn State's victims? If they can overcome the shame that accrues to abuse victims in order to seek help, it will be very expensive. And no, health insurance doesn't cover it. Abuse recovery doesn't happen in 24 visits or even 124. If I had depended only on health insurance, I'd be dead.

Over the years I've met people who did not survive, who were defeated by depression, addiction or suicide. But I know others—truly fierce people—who are recovering. And that's something else that I know is heresy in some circles: I got some gifts from my painful childhood.

The skills I use in my work today--my talents, you could say—came out of that horrible part of my life. I have a powerful intuition; the ability to anticipate what people need and feel; and so many bosses have told me that I'm "calm in a crisis" that it's funny—except when I think about how I acquired that skill.

I've seen colleagues reduced to tears over work place "problems" like losing an important file or a late proposal. For me, a woman racing through the house at 3am in a manic rage, waving a knife is a problem. Anything else is just a situation.

In a strange way I'm proud of my survival. It's a lifetime achievement. But for all the strengths I have today, I still live with too much fear and insecurity to balance this scale to the plus side.

Abuse survivors have a fierceness that rivals any elite athlete's. And my heart breaks when I think that Penn State's victims were little boys who wanted to be athletes. I hope that if they watch the Olympics this week, they will know that they have the same internal fortitude as our country's best competitors. While there are no medals and no flag ceremony for sexual abuse survivors, some of us will always be cheering for them.

Despite what the bumper sticker says, it is too late to have a happy childhood. So I take the whole package, grieve the losses, celebrate the gains and work around the scar tissue.

Happy Mother's Day Medea

If productivity is down in your workplace this week, you can blame your mother. All across the city, workers linger through their lunch hour in card stores reading and sighing. Buying Mother's Day cards is not easy.

For some, the card that says, "Mom, Thanks for being perfect" is fine, but for the rest, with complicated mothers and complicated relationships, the search for the right message is tough.

But even as children–of all ages--struggle to summarize their maternal relationship in a card, those on the receiving end have mixed feelings too. What is a good mother? Do we measure up? Most of us know we don't come close to the platitudes in the cards. On this day that celebrates kindness, patience and sacrifice, many of us squirm remembering our less than maternal moments. We wonder if we've done something really bad along the way and worry whether our worst day as a mother damaged our kids.

Mothers who hurt their children is a painful topic. The reality of mothers' hostile impulses against their children is old news in psychological circles and parenting books, but we rarely allow parents to admit those feelings. Thank goodness, most of us don't act on our thoughts, but some mothers have struggled with the limits and lost. When we hear about them, many of us know--in the privacy of our hearts--that it may be just the grace of God, good friends, a reliable baby-sitter and money in the bank that keeps us from taking their place.

So maybe we should, especially on this day, have some compassion for mothers who've lost it, or who never had the resources to begin with, those women who did the unthinkable: hurt their own child. If some mothers weren't so newsworthy for their sheer failure at mothering, the rest of us would not know where to draw the line in our self-judgment. We can count ourselves lucky and a little grateful that most of us have slapped but did not scald, screamed but did not hit, or cursed but did not kill. When we react to a child-abuse horror story with the common "Can you imagine?" the truth is that most of us can.

The "bad" mother relieves us of the shadowy fear we all carry. We owe a debt to those mothers because they give us the outside limit from which to measure our parenting. It is the bad mothers who force us to affirm our moral standards.

We can't talk about bad mothers without mentioning Medea; the mythological woman who killed her kids to punish their philandering father. But Medea got to her breaking point after a world tour of abuse, abandonment and humiliation. After being dumped in a strange country with no way home, she lost it and she killed. Medea's story is a myth but, as with all myths, it points to something real in the human psyche.

When we read about women who hurt their kids, a healthy mother has to stop and ask herself, "How did that woman get there?" Nobody starts out wanting to kill their children; nobody starts out thinking scalding is reasonable discipline.

It's baby steps all the way. Every mother who has lost it at least once, or who has done something she swore she'd never do, can be grateful for everything that keeps her from crossing over to the territory of the terrible mother.

Alexander Solzhenitsyn, Russian novelist, wrote: "If only there were evil people somewhere committing evil deeds, and we could separate them from us and destroy them, but the line dividing good and evil cuts through the heart of every human being." That includes yours and mine.

So for Mother's Day let's take a moment to thank the good mothers and to show a moment's compassion for the "Medeas" of the world, who in their tragic solution to life's problems show us where we ought not to go.

The Amy Winehouse House

A couple of weeks ago we visited a cancer support group to see what kind of help might be available. The place was lovely and there was a long list of activities for patients and caregivers. But a few minutes into the orientation I picked up the whiff of condescension that accrues around cancer.

Part of it is the pastel approach to surroundings but it's also apparent in the tone of voice that is used by staff. It's a cross between the voice you use when talking to a small child and the voice one uses talking to someone in the midst of a psychotic break. The other hint is the two-handed handshake: the staff member takes both of your hands in hers and it is accompanied by the long, deep gaze which immediately feels like someone told the staff how that "people with cancer need to be seen." And, well, they are going to make dam sure you know you are seen.

But the greatest tip-off to the fact that once you have cancer you'll never be treated like a competent adult again is revealed in the list of activities offered. The counselor took me aside to explain the caregiver activities and told me with that kindergarten teacher lilt in her voice, "We get together on Thursdays and make smoothies." Smoothies.

As I told Dave on the way home, "I have never made a smoothie in my life so why would I make smoothies in someone else's kitchen with a group of strangers because you have cancer?"

That smoothie was the turning point for me and it set me to thinking about the kind of cancer support place I'd like to create. Hence the birth of The Amy Winehouse House.

The tagline at the Amy Winehouse House is: Fuck Cancer.

Our mission: We believe that cancer and its treatment is fierce and so everything around it should meet that fierceness head on and not back down into pastel prettiness. We don't coddle and we don't play word games. We don't parse "living with" versus "dying from" cancer.

At the Amy Winehouse House we are not nice and not pastel. We don't believe that having cancer makes you nice or pastel either. If you were an ass before you got cancer, now you are an ass with cancer. We don't ask you to share, process, make crafts or drink smoothies. We offer no bookmarks or anything that has or requires a crocheted cover.

Activities at the Amy Winehouse House include: Making martinis, Strip poker night, Learning how to hot wire a car.

On Saturday nights we have strippers. Yes for girls too.

And we have a smoking room …(if you have cancer and are going to die we want you to enjoy a cigarette on us.)

And we do have drug education. We think of it as self-chemo. Our role model, Amy Winehouse, was an expert on self-chemo. Our self-chemo classes explain how to smoke crack and how to play the cancer card to score medical marijuana. Our movie nights include pornography. (After all, cancer is pornographic so why get all puppyish and pastel about something that is violent and intrusive.)

Of course we have a Board of Directors. Most nonprofits do. At The Amy Winehouse House we too have those that we turn to for guidance. These are the folks who help us stay true to the mission. So in the spirit of full disclosure here are the members of our Board:

Amy Winehouse
Keith Richards
Grace Slick
Jackson Pollock
Janice Joplin
Darryl Strawberry
Sherlock Holmes
Frances Phelan
Anna Karenina
John Falstaff
Jimmy Hendrix
Joan Kennedy

As you can imagine, planning refreshments for the Board meetings can be tricky. And, yes, we do know that some of these folks are dead. You may wonder about that, but that's kind of the point. People die of cancer so these folks are helpful on that side of things.

And yes, it has also been pointed out that some of our Board members are, in fact, "fictional." These too are important Board members. Anyone who has worked in the nonprofit world knows that these are, above all, the best kind of board members to have. You know exactly what they are going to say, and they make a lot less trouble for the staff.

Later I'll explain our policies for volunteers. We don't have tee shirts, but you do have to wear eyeliner. We'll also talk about why we hate Lance Armstrong. And yes, ...we have bracelets too, but ours say, "Fuck Cancer."

Holiday Grief

At some point each Christmas morning the telephone rings and hearing the phone I think happily, "Oh that's Lar calling to say Merry Christmas,"-- as was his habit for twenty-some years since we left home in our teens. Then smiling, rising from chair or bed to grab the phone, I drop my hand. I remember. This cannot be my brother calling; Larry is dead.

Yes, a story about death just before Christmas. It may seem wrong but it is a fact that in the midst of shopping, parties and planning, one in four Americans are also grieving this week. For many people this will be the hardest week of 2007.

Holiday grief is difficult for two reasons. This is the time of year when we focus on our loved ones. We want to send cards, buy gifts, eat together, laugh with them and maybe even fight the annual family fight. It's additionally hard because we see the rest of the world smiling with, buying for, and even complaining about, their loved ones.

Larry's death was one of several in a short time for my family. In that time I got to learn a lot from grief. One of my first lessons was that coping with holiday grief requires absolute assertiveness. The sights and sounds of the holiday can be a distraction or they can be powerfully annoying and hurtful. You don't want to take the season's joy away from others, but you may also be shocked that you can find yourself, yes a nice person like you, hating other people this time of year, strangers, even friends, simply because they still have their brother, mother, husband, child.

I know how hard this is. You may just want to cry and rage and not have to eat, shop, cook or smile. Do you dare? Bad advice from well meaning friends may be "Don't give in to grief." But I say this is the season for giving, so give in all you want, allowing grief to do its work, which is healing your heart.

But what if it's just the opposite, and Christmas, with its lights and music, has given you the first light heart you've felt all year. Do you feel disloyal or wrong somehow to be lighthearted or even laughing? No. Here's a quote from George Bernard Shaw that I keep over my desk to remind me of life's true mixtures: "Life does not cease to be funny when people die, any more than it ceases to be serious when people laugh."

So often those of us who are not in the midst of a loss don't want to see another person grieving. It scares us, I think. It's too much a reminder of our own losses felt or those yet to come. So if you are lucky enough to not be among the one in four who are grieving this week, the best gifts you can offer those who are is not glittery packages of false cheer but compassion, patience and willingness to listen.

For many years I thought the term "losing a loved one" was the worst kind of euphemism, used by people who were afraid to say the words death or dead. But when my brother Larry died, I finally understood that grief is more than an ending. Though he died years ago my general feeling about Larry is that I have misplaced him. It's that sensation of knowing that my book, glasses or that letter I was just reading is around here somewhere, if I could just remember where I left him.

I think this is why we are so hard on the grieving and why we want them to buck up. The world loves closure, loves things that are done and settled. But death and grief for all their seeming finality are not as final as we would like. This is why it is a great surprise to find that grief lasts a long time and that it contains such a range of expression.

Perhaps the most important thing I have learned from grief is that death ends a life but not a relationship. And that is why, on Christmas mornings, I still rise and reach for the phone.

It's Not the Monster That Scares Us

One of the scariest moments in the horror movie genre is when the baby-sitter gets the call telling her, " He's in the house with you!" The "he" of course, is the bad guy/murderer/monster. This week, as Halloween approaches, we'll have lots of spine chillers to entertain us. One of the classics is Frankenstein, by Mary Shelley. A best seller in 1816, and rarely out of print since, Frankenstein is probably the most beautifully written of all the scary books.

The messages of Shelley's monster classic are very much a part of our lives now. The questions that she raised so eloquently: What is life? What does it mean to be human? And where will science lead us? are as perplexing now as they were at the dawn of the scientific era. The issue of scientific intrusion into life is at the very heart of today's science news, and at the center of the proud claims of major medical and research organizations. We proclaim new ways to overcome disability, disease and death, but at what cost and to what limit? It might help us to look at Frankenstein in today's light, and take up the questions that 18-year-old Shelley was asking.

When we hear the name, Frankenstein, a common first response is the image of the lumbering, rivet headed monster immortalized by Boris Karloff.

We picture the creature assembled in the laboratory out of body parts, so ugly that humans fainted at the sight of him. This common misidentification of Frankenstein tells us how easily we tend to blame the victim and how often we overlook who the bad guy really is. In Mary Shelley's story, the large, disfigured man is named simply "The Creature." Frankenstein is not this sad man, the product of medicine and technology, but rather the scientist: Dr. Victor Frankenstein.

Shelley shows us in this story that the very tragedy of Frankenstein and what led to tragic consequences was work done in isolated obsession. Her brilliant young scientist, Dr. "F," had no association with his peers, no life outside his laboratory, nothing to balance his work.

Does this seem too much an accusation of our times? Frankenstein confesses his own dilemma: "In the year I created the Creature I had no intimacy, had not read a book, had a meal with friends, heard a concert or been to church."

Maybe that seems a little heavy handed as an admonition against work-a-holism, but how much do market competition, confidentiality and speed drive this same isolation in science today?

The second lesson in the Frankenstein story is that scientific experimentation of itself is not wrong; the trouble lies in its separation from social discourse. The issue is not to prevent creation but to take responsibility for the results. That is, to take responsibility collectively and individually for the social and human cost of new technology. Shelley's point is subtle but important: Frankenstein is a tragic figure not for experimenting but for neglecting to take responsibility for his work.

The development of new technology, particularly the integration of human and machine, is accelerating. At MIT there is a graduate program focusing on creation of "humachines." At the University of Toronto a laboratory is dedicated to Cyborg symbiosis. Do we know what "creatures" these new labs will produce? Should we be asking what these scientists are up to? Should we be asking ourselves what we want of them?

This isn't easy to dismiss with a simple "Stop tinkering." We keep reading of life-saving breakthroughs in technology and medicine. There are new possibilities for organ and limb transplants every day, it seems. Is there a line we would even think about drawing? Is a brain transplant going too far? Who decides?

Frankenstein is the perfect myth for our time, raising the question of scientific inquiry outside of dialogue about the consequences. It's so easy to point a finger at science but we find ourselves now, as consumers and patients and citizens demanding better healthcare and cures for diseases that killed our ancestors.

We don't want scientific progress to stop. But we too-- not just the scientists—must ask these old questions: What is the value of human life? What's the cost and consequence of saving one? Of making one? And who's the monster now?

Mary Shelley gives us a clue: He's in the house with us.

Accidents Happen

Remember when we were kids and we cut sharp sticks from trees to roast marshmallows and our mothers would holler at us, "Be careful with that; you could put out someone's eye out"? And on that very rare occasion, when someone did get hurt, no one sued the marshmallow company or blamed the trees. It was understood, as awful as it was, that sometimes accidents happen.

Now when we read about a tragedy in someone's home or on the road, most of us can see where the danger was and what should or shouldn't have happened. We think, "How could they have done that? "And, "I would never..."

But are we all so careful in our lives?

Yes, Oprah convinced me to stop using my cell phone in the car, but I use a tape recorder on my commute every day. I listen to books and I change the CD's while I drive. And I eat. I open candy and snacks and I twist the tops off my protein drinks –with two hands—in a moving car. I have slammed on my brakes at the last second to avoid hitting a car in front of me, and more than once I've made a left turn and been surprised by a pedestrian in the intersection. I have run with both knives and scissors. I have dropped a toddler's hand in a public place, and I've looked up from my reading to see a child in my care holding something dangerous.

A few years ago my dear friend was killed while riding her bicycle. She was hit by a car. Her death triggered a debate between cyclists and drivers. Maybe the chastisement and counterpoint made someone else safer. But her death was an accident. Terrible and horrible, but an accident.

Guns, knives, cars, bikes, swimming pools and fires. When we read about a tragedy, something happens inside of us. In the single second that it takes to realize, "My God, I could have done that," the weight of being a fallible human being is too much; we can't stand that vulnerability, that fear. So we quickly shove the thought away and seal it with an accusation. We use blame to separate ourselves.

We say, "How could he have left that out?" "How could she have done that?" "She's bad; he's negligent; there must have been something wrong with the car, or the road, or the signs"--anything rather than know, "That could be me."

The concept of an accident is abhorrent because it includes all of us.

We cannot abide the idea of accidents because accidents imply a random world and they reveal how truly powerless we are. That's too scary to accept, so we seek control in false beliefs and in blame.

We insist on a cause or someone or something to blame so that we can reassure ourselves that we still have power. We want to believe in our power at any cost. Maybe there is a correlation between our increasing sense of powerlessness and our insistence on blame. But the real cause of accidents is this: we are human beings. That may be the thing we really can't stand.

As much as we'd like to believe that we can stay safe --and alive-- forever, we can't. Yes, we'll follow the rules and think about other people's safety, but the most important lesson we can take from tragedy is to say, "I love you" to people who are dear to us, because even when we do all the right things, sometimes accidents happen.

We Have Met the Joneses and They are Us

Last year America's 100 million households each spent an average $160 a day on consumer products, adding up to 5 trillion dollars of goods and services. That's a great statistic for our economy, but for individuals the price may not be right. The number of people filing for personal bankruptcy has doubled in the last seven years and it now stands at one-and-a-half million people per year. If time is money, and money, time, then we are not just aging, we're dying.

Even if we aren't close to filing our own papers yet, most of us live too close to the line. The savings rate for the middle class is a fat zero, and most dual-earner households are living paycheck to pay check.

Who is it we are trying to please or impress with all this stuff we're buying? The old answer was the Joneses, those proverbial people next door. But, it's not the Joneses anymore.

The truth is we don't know the Joneses. Most of us are too busy working to know our neighbors. We leave in the dark and get home in the dark, so we don't see their boat or car or jewelry to covet. Sociologist Juliet Schor makes this point in her book "The Overspent American": We spend so much time at work that the people next door are no longer our reference group.

So who is? Well, we have met the Joneses and they are us. An idealized image of ourselves has replaced the neighbors as someone to identify or compete with. Without knowing actual neighbors, we are trying to define ourselves by what we see elsewhere, and that's usually in ads or on TV.

Schor's research shows that the "New Consumerism" is driven less by the pursuit of social acceptance and more by the construction of personal identity.

This change in our self-definition speaks to a greater kind of insecurity. Now, in addition to social insecurity we are also less personally secure. But our denial is high and marketers are smart. We are most susceptible to products signaling individuality.

Television, and now increased Internet use have displaced face-to-face contact as our main source of information about goods. And the time we spend watching television correlates positively with heavy spending.

We shop to declare our difference. But of course we have to be different in the right way. Is anyone willing to make their mark with a wardrobe of easy-care polyester? Ironically the consumer pursuit of individuality leads back to the catalog and the shopping mall.

Even our thought lives have this denial and duality. Every woman I know is reading the same book on how to create an authentic life. We go along reading the daily pages in lock-step; making our lists, and collecting pictures of more consumer goods in our discovery journals. Oh, I read the pink book too, but I worry: Are any of us actually authentic enough to ditch this best-selling advice and read Aristotle or Emerson instead? Or how about <u>Anna Karenina?</u> Tolstoy may have given us the best thing ever written on making choices and making a life.

Most of us would fiercely deny that we are influenced by media and ads. We insist that we're smart, we're educated, and we think for ourselves. Oh yeah? Recent consumer research shows that there is a direct correlation between greater education and the ease of persuasion by advertising. We're suckers for being told how smart we are. We buy what's being sold as long as they promise us we thought of it all by our selves.

It is just a little too easy to blame TV for the generation of our wanting. So much has been written accusing advertising for creating consumer demand. But that's not the whole story. You can lead a horse to water but you can't make him wear Hermes or drink Evian. Madison Avenue is not the all powerful and malevolent "other" who makes us want. I am at best a partner and at worst an accomplice.

Is the answer downshifting? Pulling the plug? Maybe, but it doesn't stop the shopping. There's a whole industry of "Living Simple" products and new books on how to simplify your life available for sale.

So even as we keep searching and falling short, we buy more stuff to break the fall and tell us who we are. So what can we do as we get poorer by the day? A start might be a 30-day trial. Pull the plug, but on credit cards, not the TV. Give yourself a shopping break, and look at who you really are without the mall to mirror you.

Freedom of Art

"Freedom's just another word for nothin' left to lose." Those lyrics by Kris Kristofferson were made famous by the great, gravel-voiced Janis Joplin. On the 4th of July we might hum along thinking about freedom and wondering at its costs and how much we could lose.

The fuss over artistic freedom ranges from paintings to film, to banned books to provocative movies. Michael Moore's Fahrenheit 9/11 was inspired by the sci-fi classic "Fahrenheit 451," in which Ray Bradbury described a future where art and books were banned and burned by a totalitarian government. Artists in that future responded by memorizing books, literally preserving them in their bodies.

To grasp the real-life significance of artists as political agents, we have only to remember Cambodia, Russia, Czechoslovakia and China. In those countries, as in Latin America, the first citizens sent to the gulag or the "re-education camp" were the artists. It's no coincidence that repressive governments often go after poets, painters and playwrights. The artistic sensibility and the practice of making art create a habit of asking questions and--when a political structure is fragile—the right question and one artist can bring the whole thing down. Pablo Neruda did it in Chile and Vaclav Havel was that artist in the Czech Republic.

In the United States we don't murder artists but do have culturally specific weapons for killing their work: we lower their status, minimize their contributions and cut their funding. We also belittle artists by suggesting that their opinions are irrelevant. It doesn't make sense. We accord legitimacy to attorneys and professors, and we let business leaders posit their perspectives on current affairs, but we deny that respect to those who have the most highly developed skill in sorting through rhetoric and images. Consider: Was Picasso irrelevant? Tolstoy? Dostoyevsky? Solzhenitsyn?

Solzhenitsyn's criticisms of the Soviet government were taken seriously by the United States—by the White House—as we developed our strategy and policy with the former Soviet Union. That celebrated poet and novelist said in his Nobel lecture "Art serves to battle lies and preserve the moral history of a society without the transitory and debasing rhetoric of bureaucrats."

Edward Said, the great political philosopher, wrote, "Language behaves, it follows power, but art does not behave, it stands out and stands against." Art provides contrast to the dominant messages of our culture so that we can clearly see them.

We have a wonderful example with a well-loved American artist Norman Rockwell, who used his work to comment on civic, social and political issues. His paintings for the Saturday Evening Post and Look magazine covers raised provocative questions about the impact of war, religious intolerance, civil rights and poverty in America.

Art concentrates thought and emotion. Artists see underlying truths and reflect them back to us. Artists grab us by the front of our shirts and make us look.

Right or wrong, pleasant or disturbing, they make us think. And it is thinking that is at the center of, and the true requirement for, citizenship in a democracy.

Artists ask us to see what is and to imagine what might be.

On this day when we consider those things that preserve our freedom: the laws and the wars, the courts and the candidates, we might forget that art too is part of the freedom process.

Bulletin Boards

I have a habit landlords hate. I tape things to the wall.

It began innocently enough. As a kid I kept a cork bulletin board over my desk and as I grew, the board grew with me. One day, when I reached the corner with a cluster of clippings, I did what I had to do; I turned the corner onto the wall. Now my wall is a life-sized bulletin board. Life-sized is correct; it's my life up there on the wall.

At first glance my "board" seems to be a typical source of reminders. There's a note about a dentist appointment and a scrap to remind me of a deadline. But the real function of my bulletin board is a more personal kind of reminding.

All of us look at ourselves. We look in mirrors and in the reflections of windows, but my collaged wall is also a picture of who I am at any moment. There are reviews of books to read, a sticky note that says, "Try to get a poem out of the notes on hospital weekend," a new phone number for a long-lost friend, some Amelia Earhart stamps my step-daughter gave me, and a magazine picture of a woman in a gray tweed outfit walking down the street carrying books. She looks so happy. I've had this picture for many years. I want to walk down streets like that. I want to be that happy.

There is also a picture from the Sunday New York Times magazine. It is the faculty dining room at Harvard. I saved the picture because I liked the hair of a young woman in the foreground. Her hair is natural and long and it says something to me about not chasing style, and caring more about your conversation at lunch than what your hair looks like.

There's another page up there torn from the New York Times: a picture of Jack Nicholson looking "Who me?" devilish and sexy. Rock on, Jack. There is also a very brown photo of Georgia O'Keefe: brown hat, brown kimono and she's standing under a brown sculpture called Abstraction. Her jacket is held together with a little wire brooch made for her by her friend Alexander Calder. It says "OK." Those are her initials and then some.

Also on my wall is a page from a quote-a-day calendar dated January 4, 1986. It says, "Wisdom is learning what to overlook." I meant to learn that. I really did. I still hope to.

Central on the wall is a quote that I typed on white paper many years ago. The original was a page I tore out of a mountaineering book as a teenager. Since then I've given this quote by Rene Daumal to many friends—especially when they are suffering. The words on the page say:

You cannot stay on the summit forever; you have to come down again. So why bother in the first place? Just this; what is above knows what is below but what is below does not know what is above. One climbs, one sees. One descends, one sees no longer but one has seen. There is an art to conducting oneself in the lower regions by the memory of what one saw higher up. When one can no longer see one can at least still know.

My taped up walls are reminders of things I have seen; in myself and in the world. They remind me who I am and they ask daily: Are you like this? Is this still you?

The Bambi Debate

Deer season has begun and so has the annual debate about hunting. I listen carefully to this argument because my own feelings have changed over the years. When I lived in the city, it was very easy to have disdain for hunting and hunters. But when I moved to upstate New York from Washington, DC, I got a crash course in rural living. There were wild animals in my back yard. My neighbors had dead deer hanging from porches. I was horrified. But when I learned that my neighbors depended on hunting for food, I had to examine my facile city-girl opinions.

Because I've lived on both sides of this game, I have my own totally subjective rules for who gets to play. First, if you eat meat, you don't get to debate. I mean, how arrogant can you get? If you eat steak or hamburger and you object to hunting, you are arguing about style not substance. What you are preserving is your right to act fussy and squeamish about seeing an animal carcass. Believe me, steaks and hamburgers have carcasses too.

Hunters don't get off easy in my book though: they need to clean up their language. Let's lose the word "harvest." This bizarre euphemism isn't fooling anyone. Deer are mammals, not carrots. Playing word games to obscure killing is not necessary. After all, we kill human beings all the time: in war, in our criminal justice system and with our cars. Linguistic obfuscation always heralds a lie. Remember "advisors" in Viet Nam?

One factor that confuses our debate is that we roll all hunters together when we talk about the problems. There are 750,000 registered hunters in New York, but there is no prototypical hunter. There are some, like my former neighbors, who hunt for the food their families depend on. Then there are the sportsmen who love the equipment and the ritual. There's another group for whom hunting is about having an all-guy get away with porn and beer and shooting guns. Then there are the city guys up for the weekend, who, in their Hemingway-esque fantasies, may be the most dangerous people in the woods.

Some hunters are responsible and sane, and others are rude, drunk and dangerous. We need to be specific about which hunter we are talking about when we complain, and we also need the responsible hunters to police their comrades a whole lot better.

Because I know how emotionally charged hunting talk can get, I decided to look at the essential document in this debate: I rented Bambi. There, in Disney's anti-hunting polemic, are the images that underlie our emotional conflict. I've seen this movie several times, but watching it again, I gasped when Bambi's mother is shot, and I cried at Bambi's, "Mama, where are you?" Most of us were babies when we saw this baby animal's parents get killed. You don't need Freud to analyze this.

The real issue is hard to put into words. You can hear just how inarticulate both sides become when we talk about the hunting mentality. And those who don't hunt are quick to add, "Ah, hunting is so primitive and barbaric." Well, it is, but we've got tons of leftover "barbarism" in our culture. Gardeners may be the most common "throw-back." Few of us need to grow flowers but we say, " I need to get my hands in dirt".

It's very easy to think of hunting as evil, but it's part of our nature. Wasps hunt and owls hunt, lions hunt and so do humans. When children play hide-and-seek, they are hunting, and the bargain hunter is, in fact, that.

Perhaps what troubles us most in this debate is not whether we shoot animals, but that, whether we like it or not, hunting reveals the animal in the man and the long ago past that is still at the heart of our human condition.

Labor Day

Only after having worked for many years, did I begin to understand what it must have been like for my father when the family gathered for holidays. The oldest of six brothers, my dad was an industrial engineer, an "efficiency expert" as they were called in the 1950s. He worked for the paper box company where he had worked since he was 14, the same plant where his six brothers worked the shop floor.

My father was the pride of his immigrant family; he had a college education, and he wore a tie to work. That was the dream of my uncles -- for their children. But in his success, my father had climbed not only up the stairs of the Kress Box factory; he also had climbed from labor into management.

Now, as an adult, I understand my father's dilemma, and I can admire the gracious struggle required of my uncles as they went to work, deeply proud of their older brother, yet having to deal with his stop watch and clipboard and the teasing of their coworkers.

My uncles-- and their peers-- were hard-working men. They ran heavy machines, bundled boxes by hand, and tossed thousands of pounds of corrugated paper over their heads every day. Their bodies were burned, cut, and scarred. They went to work at six in the morning and took all the overtime they could get.

Their dream for their own children was what my father had achieved: a way out of physical labor. Their work made them proud and broke their hearts.

They had the belief that poverty--and hard labor—was a plague, but that education was the vaccination against it. The jobs they were so willing to do were what they hoped their own children could avoid.

We celebrate Labor Day with these complex emotions. In every family someone did the heavy lifting so that the next generation wouldn't have to. Many of us whose forebears worked "the floor" have white-collar jobs today. The irony is that the work our grandparents did was what allowed the family's circumstances to change so that we could take the elevator-- instead of the stairs --into management.

For most of the year we ignore this paradox because we treat the working class as invisible. Though numbering in the millions, the working class has never been wholly accepted or reflected in American culture. We know the history of buildings and monuments but not who built them. Archie Bunker and Ralph Kramden are long gone, maybe because we think no one does that kind of work any more. If we gauged America by what we see on TV, we'd assume that everyone works in an office.

The American working class is invisible because we cling to a myth that America is made up of small businessmen and farmers and entrepreneurs. The persistence of this myth fails every reality test. Our good economy and position as a world leader are based on manufacturing and big industry, which demand labor. Our national self-perception denies how dependent we are on those who wear blue and pink and khaki collars to work. Those, of course, are the people who work on Labor Day: delivering papers, collecting tolls, driving buses, serving food.

Our romance with technology fuels this American fantasy. We mythologize the new gadgets and the companies that make them, but that is not the bulk of who we are, or how our work is done.

There is a man in California who lived online for one year, never leaving his house, just to prove that he could do everything using the Internet.

But on Labor Day, it's fair to ask: Who built that house, and laid those phone lines? And just who shipped the computer to his little virtual world?

In Defense of an Unbalanced Life

Over and over, almost like a mantra, so many of us are saying "I need to balance my life." Toward that end we fill our calendars outside of work with quality time with loved ones, and commitments –sometimes against the grain—to meditate or do yoga, to take classes or to volunteer. So many of us find ourselves doing little bits of lots of things and not feeling good about much of what we do.

Do you also have the nagging feeling that you can't quite get this "life balance" thing to balance? Maybe that's because it doesn't.

I realized this week that "Balance my life" is just another item on the big to-do list in my head, and it's another thing nagging at me that I should do.

Well, I quit.

I've decided that balance is overrated.

Think about it. People we admire, those who have made a difference or a contribution or who have a clear vocation lead remarkably unbalanced lives. Consider the greats in any field: Einstein? No balance at all; he was actually quite a weird guy. Thomas Edison? He never left the lab. Ditto for Marie Curie. Venus and Serena Williams? Tiger Woods? For serious athletes their entire family has to live on a tilt-a-whirl.

It's true for creative types too. Emily Dickinson? Edna St. Vincent Millay? We love their poems, but look at their lives. And statesmen? Saints? You get the idea.

So who cooked up this idea that we have to have to have our fingers in so many pies in order to have a good life? Probably writers whose own lives are notoriously out of balance. But they make it sound so simple and so wise to have a balanced life that we race around weighing and measuring to make sure we have equal parts of work, home, family, social, spiritual and civic in our lives.

The theologian Fredrick Buechner—who had a seriously unbalanced life—defines true vocation as "the place where your deep gladness meets the world's deep need." Now it doesn't make sense that deep gladness will come from ticking off a long to-do list or that the world's deep need is met by doing tiny bits of this and that like rote do-gooders.

But the idea of balance so appeals that we run faster and faster to balance our social and emotional portfolios; we take yoga and meditate, try to eat well, call friends, see the latest play, buy if not read the latest bestseller, attend the school play and send emails from the car and leave voice mail at midnight.

How much energy we waste striving to balance our lives. What if we celebrated a tilting life, one in which we gave a primary commitment to kids or business or art or spirit? Years ago when I started out as a writer I showed my plan to an experienced author. I had included a list of things that I thought belonged in a writer's life, including, "get a dog." The other writer said, "Diane, buy a picture of a dog; your job is writing."

It was good advice about making choices. Today I have two dogs, but other things had to go in the bargain.

I don't think it's balance that we really want at all. What we want is to feel good and to have peace and that mostly comes from feeling well used by life. That doesn't happen when we are running around doing little bits of many things.

Here's a radical idea for the holiday season: Give up balance; don't go to any store, party, or event unless you really want to. Give self-improvement a break. Read what you like even if it's not "good" books, and choose the couch over the gym, and the woods over the party if that is what your soul craves.

Stop and look into the world's deep need that's right here in our community. Find the source of your deep gladness that runs nearby. Allow yourself to lose your balance. And just fall in.

Death or the "D" Word

I read obituaries. I've done it for a long time. Maybe it's the writer in me who sees these death notices as tiny novels and bites of memoir. But I also read them as a spiritual practice and now, too, I read them so I can be a better citizen.

I want—as often as I can—to remind myself that I will die. Morbid? No. Or maybe yes—in the very best sense of that word. Memento mori—a reminder that death will come to me as it will to you and to everyone we know.

Why is this a political act? Because if we don't start talking about --and accepting –death, we are going to screw up health care and the economy even further.

Death and taxes. We joke about them, but those are the two things messing up our State and Federal government right now. These are two things we don't want but because we are so afraid of the first, we are doomed to more of the latter.

It matters now because we are revisiting the issue of "end of life conversations" or "death panels"—depending on your preferred political rhetoric. But you know what? It doesn't matter. Death doesn't care about rhetoric. That is what makes our denial—both the personal and the political --so silly. We have a rapidly aging population causing a huge impact on healthcare, and hence the economy, and we are like little kids with our hands over our ears saying, "La la la la la" when anyone suggests we should talk about how and when to die.

I regularly hear people my age—late 50's—saying, "Well, if I knew I was going to die then I'd..." And I think, "If? You still don't know you're going to die?"

No, I'm not looking forward to dying. There's so much
I want to do and people I love that I want more time with—
but accepting death helps with that too. Mortality is a great
values clarifier –that's why the ancients kept those skulls on
their desks.

Saving lives is in the rhetoric of every advance in healthcare. But what we miss in our excitement is that medical
advances don't save lives, they simply shift the timetable.
Here is the single most indisputable medical fact: 100% of
us are going to die. So doesn't it make sense to talk about
Death at least as much as we talk about exercise and diets
and Vitamin D?

The reality is that disease, pain and death are not necessarily things that shouldn't happen. Our bodies have to wear
out, break down or become diseased; that's how we get out
of here.

That may not necessarily be the most cheerful thought,
but there is an upside to facing death. Only when you accept
that you will die can you really decide what to do with your
life. Saul Bellow wrote, "Death is the dark backing a mirror
needs if we are to see anything." Including the "D" word—
Death—in our conversations about healthcare, we will see
more clearly and make better decisions.

Yes, healthcare is a social justice issue. We need to ask:
What can we do for the most and the many? What would
compassion aligned with reality look like? Even though ultimately the decisions will be made on a political level, that's
not where the conversation begins. If we want our values
reflected in our healthcare and our economy then we, each
of us, have to start talking about dying.

So Pretty

There's a story we tell in my family about my niece Sharon. When Sharon was a toddler, maybe three or four years old, her parents brought her home to Pittsburgh for a visit. One of the attractions in our neighborhood was the Pittsburgh Aviary, a beautiful glass pavilion filled with exotic birds.

That Saturday morning we took Sharon to see the birds. The adults spent most of their time visiting and talking while the kids wandered through the rooms of tropical plants. I was supposed to be watching Sharon but I got waylaid, and when I looked up she was gone.

I ran to look for her, hurrying through rooms of peacocks and cockatoos, and finally, I saw her in a room just ahead. I stopped to watch her. Sharon was standing in front of a birdcage. It was the Aviary's talking parrot. He was no big deal; he only knew how to say one thing. He kept repeating, "You're so pretty".

And there in front of the parrot was Sharon, standing with her little hands folded demurely in front of her, chin dropped coquettishly to one side, her eyes lowered, and she was saying over and over, "Oh, thank you. Oh, thank you."

I thought about Sharon's story recently when I went to a fancy beauty salon for a make-up lesson. Trish, the make-up artist, had been recommended by a friend. So I spent the morning swathed in pink, listening intently as Trish coached while her hands swirled in front of my face. We spent almost two hours going through all the tiny pots and tubes on her counter. Trish recommended a lip mask, special scrub vitamins and a four-part nighttime procedure. ...dred and sixty dollars later I had a made-over face, a tote bag of new make-up and some tricks to try at home. This wasn't the first time I've done this. Over the years I've had makeovers in department stores and done a few of those at-home skincare parties with friends. I always buy something. Once I even signed on for the Erno Lazlo line. I actually became a member. Lazlo won't just sell you their special black soap unless you take an oath – and pay $175.

I've even had my colors done. That cost $125. I was draped in silver and gold lame while bright lights were shined in my eyes. After much meditation and deep thought, Suzanne, the "color consultant" declared, "Yes, you are definitely a Spring."

I emerged from her studio with a swatch book for my "Spring" diagnosis. I had fabric samples in the muted tones that a "spring" like me should wear. That day I went to an outlet and bought $200 worth of cotton turtlenecks and spent $100 on scarves in my new colors. I was getting smarter. I wasn't going to buy a whole new wardrobe so I got these things to make my old clothes "right." A one day total of $375 for "Spring" training.

A month later, a colleague at work, a color consultant herself, caught me wearing what I knew to be a "wrong" color – a bright green blouse. "Yes", she exclaimed, "That's really you, you're a perfect 'Winter.'

But I did expect a better reaction last week when I came home from Trish's salon to meet my husband for lunch. I was pleased with my rose shadow, amber crease color, and navy mascara. When I took off my sunglasses, my husband looked up from his salad and said, "Hi. What happened to your eyes?"

That's not what they said at the salon where Trish works. After she had finished my makeover, Trish, and all of her coworkers--and even the lady who took my check-- said, "You look so pretty."

I simply said, "Oh, Thank you."

The Demise of the Double Stick Popsicle

When I was growing up in the early 1950s the true test and measure of a friendship was the double-stick Popsicle. Though fall and winter were times when kids shared books and games and solicited friendship through notes passed in class, the real bonds of those relationships were forged in warm weather. The strength of a friendship's bond was challenged whenever two kids each pitched in three cents, (later five cents each) to split a Popsicle.

So when I heard that Gold Bond Ice Cream was discontinuing the double-stick confection, I panicked. But a call to the firm's marketing division assured me that the "twins," while long gone from the grocery stores, would still be available in convenience stores.

What a relief. Losing the double stick Popsicle would be much more than just the passing of another childhood memory. A single stick ice treat speaks to new social views and a new style of relationship among young friends. The double-stick Popsicle was a ritual and test of friendship.

Choosing the flavor was the first decision. You were really choosing the color--the flavor was always the same –cold and sweet. But everyone had a preference: blue, red, grape or chocolate. (Yes, there were chocolate popsicles that spoiled many a child's pastel play clothes.) Dominance in the relationship was shown by the color choice. Would you insist on blue, while she chose red? And who won? Or would you both settle for orange, which seemed to be no one's true favorite, existing only as the compromise choice?

Once the flavor/color was settled and everyone noted the assertiveness shift in the relationship, the important challenge of the double stick treat awaited. It had to be broken in half. The indentation, not quite a crease, was the indication of where it was to be divided.

But how was another decision. You could slap it against the edge of a counter or on the corner of a building, or, if you were near home, you could dash into the house to stab the Popsicle with a dinner knife to pry the halves apart. The usual method was the thumb press: thumbs push in, fingers pull back. But you had to decide who would do the breaking. Was the chief criterion strength? experience? finesse?

With a clean break each friend walked away with one-half of the treat on his own stick. If disaster struck, there was an immediate friendship test. When the Popsicle broke on the horizontal, who got the bottom with two sticks and who received –or volunteered for –the top half, with two sicle nubs to be eaten out of the wrapper? You could tell at six who would grow up to be a martyr.

And then how did two friends who had jointly purchased this cold, colorful dessert deal with the wrapper issue? For several years the Popsicle company offered gifts and prizes in exchange for a number of the red sicle balls carefully cut from the wrappers. By sending in 10 to 20 red sicle balls and enclosing a quarter you could get joke books, jump ropes or (for a brief time) small metal airplanes. Did you flip a coin for the wrapper, argue over who got it last time or each make a case for need?

These dilemmas and decisions of dealing with the double stick Popsicle taught kids the basics of negotiation and joint custody. Sharing a double Popsicle was a true test and mark of friendship. The single stick now replaces it. And with that proud, icy independence, something is lost.

Understanding Canada

We were on vacation in Northern Ontario. It was midnight in the little village and no cars had moved for hours. At the crosswalk I step into the intersection and feel a sudden tug on my arm. As Peter pulls me back to the curb, I look up to see that the signal says, "Don't Walk." Smiling I stand on the silent sidewalk and wait. When the traffic signal glows its approval to cross we step out carefully and correctly; I laugh. This is the kind of thing that happens in a mixed marriage. I married a Canadian.

Hockey, beer, donuts, moose –these stereotypes, all rooted in Canadian reality are funny to Americans. We especially like the accent, the lilting up and down of Canadian speech. In just a few hours in Ontario I am imitating my in-laws, "Will ya go to the lake, eh?" But I also know that the final "eh" on Canadian sentences and obeying traffic signals are related. The Canadian "eh" is not just a conversational tic. That uplifting extra syllable is an invitation to consensus, to agreement, and to keeping the order.

Keeping order is one of the greater aspects of Canada that we Americans-- so nearby-- miss when we think "Canadian." Canadians –motivated by a concern for a "common good" are more orderly, law abiding and considerate than we. It's not because they are nicer, but consideration of one's impact on others is a strong cultural value.

Speech patterns give more than a clue to this difference. The histories of our nations are echoed in how we use our common language. There are very few declarations in Cana-

dian dialect. Declarations invite challenge. This makes sense
when you remember that Canada did not have to struggle
for independence as Americans did. Britain approved Canada's confederation in 1867. So you can hear how the in-
flection, that final "eh," leaves the conversational door open
with space for another's thought.

For example, while visiting, we met a young man who
was dating a niece. He was not as bright as the family might
have liked. But as I was about to blurt, in my American de-
clarative, "He's an idiot", my sister-in-law said in her Canadian lilt, "Ya say hello to him and he's stuck for an answer,
eh?" Message delivered; door left ajar.

Americans however are poised for a fight. You can hear
it in our speech with its tone of certainty and downward in-
flection; we are always staking a conversational claim. Even
the most pacifist of us holds our opinions –and our right to
them—like guns. This also comes from our past. We arrived
here fighting.

This is also why the gun control issue seems easier to
Canadians. Friends in Ontario shake their heads at our de-
bates and say, "Such a big fuss, eh?" For us the gun question
is emotionally charged because at a deep level we remember
fighting for our land and freedom.

It may be around the idea of freedom that our look-alike
cultures diverge. Peter and I have a regular debate about freedom. I say Americans have more freedom: We can be and do
and say whatever we like. It's freedom TO. But, says Peter, in
Canada freedom is seen as freedom FROM. The Canadian
consideration for the common good allows Canadians relative freedom from violence, from crime, and from poverty.

Because Canada is a non-litigious culture, Canadians are
especially free of the kinds of legal hassles that cost Ameri-

cans so much time and money, and that require our hot, take-out coffee to be labeled "Hot Coffee," Duh.

These differences run deep but they're obvious when you lay the historic values side by side. We salute "Life, Liberty and the Pursuit of Happiness." There is a win-the-West, win-the-war feel to it. Then picture Canada's: "Peace, Order and Good Government." Can't you just see people queuing up and taking turns, and leaving room in the conversation for the other guy?

Canada is not a land of Boy Scout, do-gooders of course. The very contradictions make you love 'em, eh? Theirs is a mostly non-violent culture whose national pastime—hockey-- knocks the teeth out of every male over nine years of age. And while living surrounded by natural beauty and wilderness air, Canadians smoke themselves to death. We joke that Canadian restaurants offer two seating choices: Smoking and Chain-Smoking.

Having a Canadian family, I have learned a lot. I've learned to care more about the rest of the world as Canadians do and to not run from the room when the world news comes on. I've learned that waiting for the walk signal is not passive submission to rules and regs. Rather it's an active expression of community and of being part of the common good.

Lois Wilson and Alanon

March 4th is a special day to millions of people in 12 step programs. It is the birthday of Lois Wilson, who might, with great affection, be called the most famous co-dependent. She was the wife of Bill Wilson, co-founder of Alcoholics Anonymous. Their story is chronicled in AA history books.

It was Ebby T., son of a prominent Albany family, who first "carried the message" to a very deteriorated Bill Wilson. The message Ebby brought to Bill and Lois was that he had gotten sober through the help of the Oxford Group, an evangelical Christian movement. The six steps of reformation in the Oxford Group were the forerunner of today's 12 steps.

At Ebby's urging, Lois and Bill began to attend Oxford Group meetings and a few months later, on a trip to Akron, Bill reached out to members there and met Dr. Bob Smith. From the date of their meeting--one drinker helping another--we date the birth of Alcoholics Anonymous.

Those early meetings were held in private homes. Wives accompanied their husbands and took charge of the refreshments. While the men coached each other through confession and repentance in the parlor, the wives sat in the kitchen, confessing their own frustrations as they discovered the common impact that alcohol had on their families.

To her dismay, Lois later wrote, Bill's sobriety didn't bring the happiness she expected. While he was drinking, Lois had played a central if troubled role in Bill's life. Now, as he recovered she felt less important. This resentment over Bill finally achieving sobriety without her help troubled Lois.

She and other wives, who had lived on the edge emotionally and financially, realized that the 12 steps "could also work for the wives."

Every organization has history and myth. History tells us that the very first meetings in which the wives of alcoholics began to study the 12 steps began in San Francisco, but the myth, always more powerful, says that Lois Wilson began the program in New York.

The truth is somewhere in the middle. All over the country, as AA grew, it was women who often were first to seek help for their families. Lois and other wives offered support and promoted a spiritual program. At conventions Lois took the podium to tell her side of the Wilson family story, sharing with humor the lengths she went to control Bill's drinking and the humiliation she endured as she realized she could not.

As Bill W. took on the role of father of AA, it added a nice symmetry to have Lois as the mother of Al-Anon. Positioning Lois atop the recovery pantheon was strategic; she was a doctor's daughter, with a college education. Lois gave a respectable face to a problem that was shameful and secretive.

In 1957 Al-Anon gained broad public recognition when Lois Wilson appeared on the Loretta Young television show bringing the problem of alcoholism and its impact on the family directly into America's living rooms.

But there is always danger when one is placed on a pedestal. Lois was criticized because she couldn't do in her own home what she advocated for others: setting limits on bad behavior. While Bill did stay sober for many years, he was also a chronic womanizer. The fact of his adultery was made public when in his will, he left part of the royalties from "the Big Book," AA's text, to his last mistress.

It may be that in this very personal and painful way Lois Wilson left us her legacy of recovery. Al-Anon with its mission of respectability for families affected by alcoholism, has today more than 30,000 groups in 100 countries. She also, by her graceful life and the imperfection in her marriage, gave us an embodiment of AA's slogan, "progress not perfection." Thank you, Lois.

Who Are Your References?

Many people are looking for jobs right now. New technologies and social networks make it both easier and harder. Those who are hiring struggle too. Can you get a true sense of someone in 60 minutes? Can you gauge a good fit from a resume?

The best interview questions I've been asked and then learned to ask others are, "What is intolerable to you?" and "What will we know about you in six months that we could not know now?" These reveal character and one's level of self-awareness. Success later, when the daily stuff of a workplace happens—and stuff always happens-- will depend on those two factors.

Yes, you'll get references, but when you call around you don't really find out who a person is and how well they'll fit in. The important factor may not be who someone knows but whom they know about.

Ever since I was a kid I've loved biographies. I treasured my "We Were There" books that told the personal stories of historic figures. I loved learning how people lived inside their lives not just what they did on the outside.

I still do this for both inspiration and comfort. Reading about how famous folks live behind closed doors helps me to get a clearer picture of myself and others.

A perfect example is Katherine Hepburn. As an actress she was celebrated for her strength and independence, her single life and chic trousers taken as symbols of strength that women tortured themselves with by comparison. "Why can't I be like Katherine Hepburn?" But after her death we learned that Hepburn was fragile. She was in a deeply codependent relationship with a married Spencer Tracy, collapsing under his criticism, changing her every appointment, hairstyle and opinion to please him.

Joe DiMaggio is another. Known as the quintessential strong, silent guy, it turned out that DiMaggio was not elegantly elusive but scared, controlling and always fearful that his childhood poverty would return. These larger-than-life people had faults, eccentricities, and problems. Famous people—and the rest of us--are "broken in the wheels of living;" the phrase Thornton Wilder used to describe the human condition. It turns out that Katherine Hepburn wasn't really "Katherine Hepburn." Ditto for DiMaggio, Gandhi or Martin Luther King, Jr.

Now I'm reading about Dorothy Day, founder of the Catholic Worker movement. She was a writer, social justice advocate and a woman of paradox and complexity. She was devoutly Catholic, and she had a child outside of marriage. She read the gospels and the Russian novelists, and she went to confession and the opera on a regular basis. She took from the rich –including the Church--to give to the poor and she loved beautiful clothes and wore them well. What inspired me was learning about how she managed her insides. Psychiatrist and author Robert Coles, who knew Day, said:

Instead of rules she had deep references. Because she could make choices with constant inner references to the gospel or a great thinker like Dostoevsky, she could land in the same place over and over again.

This idea of inner references suggests a new job interview question. What if we asked about references but with a new spin.

What if we said, "Tell me about your references; who do you carry inside you to enlarge your moral imagination?" Who do you read about and learn from? The best references are not people who know us but those whom we want to know better. Do you know yours? Who are your references?

The Real Political Scene is in the Office

We are in a recession—or we're not. Things are getting better—or they're not. We don't know whether to get our hopes up or to hunker down. Both the national and state politics are scary. But it's the political scene we enter tomorrow morning that will keep most of us tossing and turning tonight.

Office politics. Those are the hardest politics we face—and now made even harder by budget cuts and union battles.

A young friend recently said to me, "I don't want to work where there are politics." I understood her distress, but I said to her, "Then go home and make pot holders." There is no work without politics because there is no work without people. Any time we organize ourselves into a business, a women's club, a church group or a scout troop, there will be politics.

The trend toward making the workplace feel like home doesn't help. By loosening the home and work boundary we get to have—at work—all the goodies that belong at home: sibling rivalry, parental intrusion, and fights about money, cleaning and table manners. Maybe if work were less like home we'd go home to get the things we're supposed to get there: love, companionship and intimacy.

Another complication we add at work is using the word "team." I know it's supposed to be a metaphor but then we forget what really happens on teams: hierarchy, competition and rivalry. Did you watch March Madness? Then you saw great teams –and great coaches-- and a lot of sweating and swearing and glaring.

So it's inevitable that we have office politics. Every day each of us carries our emotional baggage to work in an invisible tote bag and then we pick from it throughout the day. But this is not necessarily a bad thing. Working with other human beings is a creative process—and a messy one. Maybe the best we can do is to try not to draw blood and to say we're sorry when we do. But like the sign says in the casino, "You must be present to win," we need the politics in our workplaces and in our communities to work out who we are and how we get better.

I'm an optimist. I see the messiness of human beings as a good thing. You might roll your eyes and call me a "Pollyanna," but that fictional girl is not a bad role model. The Dali Lama has little on the 11-year-old girl that Eleanor Porter created in 1912. Pollyanna is the story of a girl who went through many painful events with very difficult people and was able to remain optimistic and make changes for the good.

Pollyanna lived in poverty, was orphaned, treated poorly and had illness and grief in her life. It's not that she didn't feel pain rather she chose to see the world as a good place despite the suffering. While most of us adults know how to toughen up in order to survive, Pollyanna's talent was in dealing with all of the difficulties while keeping her heart open.

It can feel safer to stay with the negative, but pessimism is lazy. You can always be somewhat right. To stay optimistic takes courage. You have to keep believing that things will work out even if it's not the way you hoped they would.

Now in our nation, our state and our workplaces we get to make that choice. We can moan and groan, or choose optimism. That may just be the smartest political strategy of all.

We are Easter People

I have an Easter memory from years ago. I was living in Washington, DC, and that year was a low point in my life. My older sister had recently died and both of my brothers were seriously ill; my best friend was leaving town, and on top of that I was questioning my work.

In my journal that April I wrote, "Am I depressed?" When I read those pages now, I laugh and shake my head. "Depressed?" That I even had to ask. In that long year I thought I'd never laugh again, just as I thought I'd never again feel love, the joy of easy friendship, or the satisfaction of good work.

I went to church that Easter out of both habit and desperation. I had grown up in a church-going family. It was what we did. And so to honor the family that I was losing, I went.

I chose a big downtown church for Easter services—one with hundreds in the congregation--not daring to visit a smaller church where I might have to speak to people or be embarrassed by my own tears. I wanted the paradoxical safety and anonymity of being in a crowd.

The minister that Easter Sunday said many things that I don't remember, but one sentence has stayed with me all these years. He said, "We live in a Good Friday world..."

That I understood. A Good Friday world is a world full of suffering, questioning, unfairness, trouble, mistakes, hurts, losses and grief. That was certainly confirmation of my life that day.

"But," he continued, "we are Easter people." Those words stopped me cold. I was stunned to be reminded that painful morning that there was something other than what I was feeling.

My life was not instantly transformed; his words did not change the course of my brothers' illnesses, nor give me answers to my questions. But the idea of being "Easter people" gave me a pause in my grief and the teeniest hope that there really did exist something other than pain.

Today all of the things that hurt so much back then have changed. As my brothers died, friends came forward to help. I began to write and publish. Months later I moved to upstate New York and a new life began with new love, new friends, new work and yes, of course, new problems.

What strikes me now is that this believing in "Easter" in the midst of "Good Friday" is as much about being an American as it is about being Christian. Americans are, by character, a people of reinvention. There is an extra layer of intention that we bring to "new life" that isn't true even in other predominately Christian cultures. As Americans we are future oriented, we look forward not back, and we are, for the most part, a culture of optimistic, hopeful people.

Our American value of reinvention shows itself in our politics and our policies, in our laws and in our myths. Even in our entertainment. We believe in treatment and rehabilitation. We invest in cures and self-improvement. We celebrate ambition and promotion. Sometimes we carry it too far, with too much changing partners and plastic surgery--but at the core is our belief that we can make ourselves over.

The gift from that Easter service many years ago was the reminder that we are, by religion or culture, a people who believe in possibility. When our hearts are shattered we are sometimes shocked to discover that there is joy as well as pain inside.

Out of the ashes of our mistakes, from our defeats and even our despair, we rise again in better lives.

In the Deep End on Father's Day

He was there at the end of the diving board. He would tread water for hours waiting and watching while I practiced my dives. For many years this was our Sunday afternoon ritual and delight.

My father would tread water, waiting off to one side. He would give me the sign that it was OK to dive, and I would stroll to the end of the board, tugging my stretchy lavender swimsuit, and bounce in the air before I dove in.

I would rise to the surface sputtering, and look for his face. He would hesitate a moment to let me right myself, and I would cough and beam. He would grab the back of my suit and give me a push toward the side. "Swim to the ladder," he would say, and he would stay out at the end of the diving board waiting.

I remember the feeling as I paddled to the ladder. The world was perfect: I was diving in the deep end of the pool. There was no pain or need in my life. I was a perfect, grinning, sunburned, water-logged four-year-old, in love with the world, herself and her daddy.

He died when I was 18. A lot happened in those years in-between. By the time I was 13, my father was traveling a lot and when we did spend the occasional weekend together we did not speak of personal things. As a teenager I felt awkward with my father, so I would interview him about his job. He would respond with stories about work, grateful to have something comfortable to talk about. I know a lot about industrial engineering. It filled our time.

On a July evening, when he was 55 years old, my father had a stroke and died.

It's been so many years and I still wrestle with those two men--the daddy who waited in the deep water and the man who left suddenly, without a word, when I was 18. Somewhere inside of me the four-year-old still wears her lavender swimsuit. She's at the end of a diving board, leaning forward trying to hear someone say, "You are so special." There is an ache for those words.

Romance, of course, is a way to meet that need. But romance has its own path and letting a four-year-old twirl in a 54-year-old body begins to cost too much. There is too much twirling for fewer and fewer precious affirmations, and other people along that dervish path get hurt. But when the four-year-old is anxious, we search on, even knowing that no matter what you do in the present, you cannot fill a hole that exists in the past.

Early death isn't the only way that fathers go missing. Some dads disappear into addiction or alcoholism, some to depression or divorce, and some to just working too much.

So what is my gift that I have from a father who left when we were both too young? It's this: For a long time I resented the missing memories; no father-daughter chats, no drives to college, no adult conversations. But I have this other thing—a picture in my head of my father in the water at the end of the board. It's a spiritual gift from the father who loved me but who left without talking. Today I believe in a God who looks around my life and says, "Hold on a minute." Today there is a God at the end of my daily diving board who says to me, "Okay now, catch your breath. I'm here."

Are You Old Enough for the Opera?

Picture this: Your life has just gone down the drain. So you swallow a lethal dose of poison. Just as your nervous system begins to fail, you sing a moving and beautiful song. Crazy? Not at all; just another night at the opera!

Yes, it is opera season in upstate New York, and we are lucky to have some of the best opera in the world so close by. To the north, we have the Lake George Opera, the oldest opera festival in the US, and to the west, the world-class Glimmerglass Opera.

As an opera fan I'm used to hearing, "How can you like opera? Isn't it contrived?" Younger people, especially, complain that opera is unrealistic: "Who sings when they are dying?" I know they imagine, as I once did, that opera is for the stodgy or the rich. It is true that opera isn't for everyone. Opera is an acquired taste. But that is because, to appreciate opera, you must first acquire some life experience.

This, more than any other reason, is why opera audiences tend to be older. On first glance it may seem that this is the group that can afford the tickets, but in fact the age of opera's audience reflects experience rather than age alone. There are some young people who are old enough for the opera. So how do you know if you're ready? It all depends on your story.

Opera is all about story. Its basic appeal is that it is a story told in song. We're attracted to good stories because stories are how we teach and how we learn. The old saying is true: A smart man learns from his own experience but wise man learns from someone else's. This is why we tell tales, why we gossip and why we go to the opera.

But critics say, "Oh, the stories of opera are so old, who can relate?" Yes, opera does have deep roots going back to ancient Greek theater, but the stories are timeless. The plots of opera's standard repertory read like headlines from yesterday's New York Post: "Disgruntled Bozo Snaps. Stabs Two" (Pagliacci) or "Seamstress Coughs To Death As Friends Look On" (La Boheme) or "Bride Goes Mad; Murders Hubby On Honeymoon" (Lucia di Lammermoor) or "Daughter Of Court Official Murdered; Father Left Holding The Bag" (Rigoletto)

I didn't always love the opera. I remember the very first time I went. I was in my twenties. It was something German, Wagner probably, and I remember the night was long and I was bored. So what changed? I got older and life began to happen. When I look back at that time in my twenties I realize that I hadn't yet begun and ended my first marriage and didn't fully understand the concept of tragi-comedy. I hadn't yet had the experience of seeing people I loved dying and learned that singing is the least of the strange things people do on their death beds. And in my twenties I hadn't yet had a serious illness of my own so I hadn't learned that sweet and scary amalgam of fear, self-pity, courage and melodrama.

But what about all that singing? People don't really sing about their problems do they? Well, ask yourself: Have you ever had a really bad day and found that talking didn't help, but when you drove up the Northway singing "Take This Job And Shove It" you felt better when you got home? Or maybe the day after a break-up you couldn't move the gray knot lodged in your gut but a song on the radio helped you to cry and get those feelings moving.

So how can you know if you're old enough? Here's my theory on what it takes to understand and love opera. You have to have lived a little and loved a lot. So, ask yourself: Have you ever, against your own good sense, and your best friend's advice, fallen for the wrong person? Do you know, despite the false comfort we offer teenagers, that sometimes unrequited lovers do suffer for years? Have you ever begged God to stop an illness, a death or someone else's decision? And have you learned that forgiveness doesn't follow a formula and that it can come like grace after something as simple as hearing a song? Finally, have you learned that not only can you laugh until you cry (youngsters do that) but that it's also possible, when things get really bad, to cry so hard you'll finally laugh?

When you are old enough and have hurt enough and you know just how strange life can be, opera doesn't seem silly at all. If you know from first-hand experience that grief and humor are the two lines running parallel down the center of life's highway, then you too are old enough to go to the opera.

The Power of One

I've noticed recently that in some social situations there is a subtle inquiry taking place. It often begins with a comment like, "Boy do we need to make some changes in the world." This seemingly benign conversation opener is a way that many of us are discreetly searching for our comrades. Those who are sad at the prospect of where we are headed have become careful—almost paranoid—not to broadcast our Liberal leanings. We're outnumbered and afraid.

But once we've confirmed that we've met a fellow sufferer, we ask, "What do we do now?" Our worry is related to the anticipated erosion of the economy, civil liberties, reproductive rights, medical advances and peace in the world.

When I hear, "What do we do now?" I understand the angst. I've been telling friends that I'm going to join the underground cell. I'm only half joking. For the first time I have a visceral understanding of how fear and frustration can get someone to that edge of bad judgment.

But I have also begun to have second thoughts about the "What do we do now?" question. While it's asked out of a desire for comfort and guidance, the truth is that maybe what's needed is not what we should do but more of what "I" and "you" should do now.

Yes, we're sad and depressed. We assume that our options are to either take Prozac or take action. We're considering political strategies, protests, more committees and always more fund raising. But maybe there is something less direct but ultimately more effective that we should consider.

What has prompted my thinking is the story of John Wollman. Wollman was an American Quaker who lived in the 1700's. He's best known for his journal, a literary treasure, but his most memorable accomplishment came from asking simple questions.

In the 18th century many Quakers were wealthy and conservative slave owners. John Wollman had concerns with that practice, and so he spent 20 years visiting Quakers up and down the East Coast. Wollman didn't preach or criticize their ways but instead asked: "What does it mean to be a moral person?" "What does it mean to own a human being?" and "What does it mean to will a slave to one's children?"

By 1770, a century before the Civil War, not one Quaker owned a slave. The Quakers became the first religious group to denounce and renounce slavery.

Wollman's story shows that simple questions—even without answers--can have a profound impact.

This may be one of those times when each of us needs to question larger societal issues where and when they touch us. Just imagine what it would be like if each of us, in our own home, neighborhood or workplace asked simple questions or stated our concerns simply, decently and directly. What if we just asked why? Or clearly said, "That's not OK" when we saw something troubling. We would not need signs or protests or petitions. We would not need to criticize anyone else or their beliefs.

Just imagine some of these scenarios: Does your company provide health coverage for domestic partnerships? Offer family leave? Pay a living wage to entry-level employees? What if you simply asked why not? Or said out loud in just one meeting said, "That's not OK."

Think about the power of John Wollman's questions and how he changed slavery. Then imagine the impact of one person not laughing at a racist joke, not smiling at a sexist remark, or asking why things are the way they are for certain people in our community.

Will I see you at the revolution? We won't need banners or bullhorns. The song says, "Let there be peace on earth, and let it begin with me." But maybe justice, integrity and democracy have to begin with me too.

Roberto Clemente

In the same way that Americans of a certain age will say to each other, "Where were you when Kennedy was shot?" baseball fans will ask one another, "Where were you when you heard that Roberto Clemente died?"

Roberto Clemente was that important--to Pittsburgh and to baseball, and to the world of sports and beyond.

As we end this year, one that has seen money and drugs foul the world of baseball, we can remember a ball player who allowed us to see athletes as honorable. The word "hero" is often misused—especially in sports--but the true meaning is "one who gives his life to help others," and that is what Clemente did on December 31, 1972, thirty-five years ago today.

Roberto Clemente died that night in a plane crash en route to Nicaragua, bringing relief supplies to victims of an earthquake. He was 38 years old.

Clemente is remembered as one of the best arms in baseball. Many believe he was the greatest right-fielder ever, shining in the outfield, tracking down every ball in range, often making spectacular leaping and diving catches. And then there was that throw—all the catcher had to do was stand there.

Known as "The Great One," Clemente's lifetime batting average was .317. He earned four National League batting championships, twelve Gold Glove awards, and was National League MVP in 1966 and World Series MVP in 1971. He was the first Latin American player elected to the Baseball Hall of Fame. In addition to his hard work on the field, Clemente worked between games and in the off-season helping the poor and visiting sick children in every major league city. He did none of it for media attention.

Bob Prince, colorful announcer for the Pittsburgh Pirates, used to sing out, "Arriba!" when Clemente came up to bat. In Spanish arriba means "get going" or "get there," and Clemente could get there. December 31, 1972, he was going to Nicaragua to ensure that the relief supplies he gathered would reach the starving victims.

The qualities mentioned by those who played with Clemente or who saw him play are pride, fury, grace and always dignity. The poet, Enrique Zorilla, wrote: "What burned in the cheeks of Roberto Clemente was the fire of dignity."

On September 30, 1972 Clemente drove a double off Met pitcher Jon Matlack for his 3,000 career hit. Three months later, on New Year's Eve, his life ended when the plane crashed into the Atlantic Ocean. There were no survivors.

Even if you care nothing for baseball, or even if you are a Yankee fan who still cringes at the mention of 1960, you can borrow from Clemente's legacy as you consider your New Year's resolutions. Roberto Clemente often said, "Any time you have the opportunity to make a difference in this world and you don't do it, you are wasting your time on this earth."

In Spanish, Clemente means merciful. He lived up to his name.

Branch Rickey

In 1947 Jackie Robinson ran onto Ebbets Field, taking his place at first base and in baseball history. But history rarely happens in single moments and almost never by individuals working alone. There were others behind Robinson who made it possible for him to take that courageous step, and this week there's a new book detailing another hero of that important day.

Legendary reporter and Pulitzer Prize winner, Jimmy Breslin has a new book about Branch Rickey--the man who got the ball rolling four years before Jackie Robinson stepped on first base. Rickey, the president of the Brooklyn Dodgers, had been managing baseball teams nearly all of his adult life and when he came to the Dodgers, he inherited an aging team, a declining audience and a big deficit. Rickey knew that the hottest talent in baseball at that time was in The Negro National League and he knew that the audience for those games, while mostly black, included many white fans who loved the tough and exciting brand of baseball played by black teams. A smart businessman, Rickey knew that Black baseball was a multi-million dollar enterprise, while his Dodgers' ledger was inked in red every day.

But in addition to being a smart and competitive businessman, Rickey was also a man of integrity and compassion who had hated racism all of his life. At age 64, Rickey's decision to break the color line in major league ball was in equal measure a choice for social justice and to win a pennant and make some money.

Ultimately, it was Jackie Robinson who stepped onto Ebbets Field April 15th 1947, and we know the punishment he had to take for doing that. Robinson lived by Rickey's terms and they were tough. Rickey made Robinson promise, "No reaction, no matter what" for three years. He put up with bean balls aimed at his head, spikes aimed at his shins and the ugly names aimed at him and his family. Rickey later wrote that "Jackie had to turn the other cheek so often he had no other cheek left—both were beaten off."

But for Rickey the consequence of spending years to orchestrate Robinson's entry, and for at least the ten years after, was having ferocious battles of his own. Rickey lost friends, and his family too endured the scorn and punishment of most major league owners and managers and players.

Breslin's new book, "Branch Rickey: An American Life," tells a classic American bootstrap story. With belief in hard work and faith in God and in the equality of all men, Branch Rickey climbed from poverty to success in the quintessential American industry: Baseball. Breslin's book shows us that when we talk about Jackie's courage, we have to acknowledge Rickey's courage too.

Robinson is, of course, a role model, for anyone who has to face being a "first", but Branch Rickey is also a model showing us that making a profit doesn't have to be separate from making social change.

Few of us will have the opportunity to enact history in the dramatic way that Jackie Robinson did, but we all have opportunities to be like Branch Rickey who ensured the moment could happen.

Now, as our State and nation struggle to improve how people live and we're looking to business leaders and the corporate world for help, Rickey shows us that making a profit and social justice can be integrated.

Rickey and Robinson are proof that it's possible to do well and do good at the same time.

Day of the Dead

Today I celebrate Dia de los Muertos, or Day of the Dead. It's not a holiday I grew up with but one I've borrowed from the Southwest and Mexico. It's become one of my favorite holidays partly because it's a good spiritual counterpart to Halloween. Except for the candy, October 31ˢᵗ doesn't leave much for grownups. Being scared of goblins and ghoulies lost its sway when I got old enough to lose people that I loved. The dead just aren't scary in the same way anymore. I'm not spooked by the idea of ghosts now; in fact, I'd welcome a visit from some of them.

That's what Day of the Dead is about. There is a belief that on this day the veil separating this world and the next is thinner, and so it's a time we can be closer to those that we love who have died.

Day of the Dead celebration centers on rituals for remembering loved ones and our relationship with them. We can visit in our imagination or feel their presence. It can mean prayer or conversation, writing a letter or looking at old photos. The Mexican tradition that I use includes making an ofrenda, or altar, something as simple as putting photos and candles on the coffee table and taking time to talk and remember. We also have chocolate as a symbol of the sweet and bitter separation from those we love.

A ritual is a way of ordering life. Whether Purim or Advent, hearing Mass or saying Kaddish, small ceremonies help us sort and reframe our memories. When someone dies, the relationship doesn't stop, it's renegotiated, literally re-conceived.

This isn't a very American idea. Culturally our prefer-ences are for efficiency and effectiveness; even with grief we use words like closure and process.

I remember my frustration when I was grieving and well-intentioned friends would suggest I move along in my process and quoted Elizabeth Kubler-Ross. The simplified version of her theory lists stages: Denial--Bargaining--Anger--Depres-sion, and Acceptance. But it's false to create an expectation of five discreet steps. This listing implies order and implies that a person can move from point A to point B and be done. That makes grief seem like an emotional Monopoly game where you go around the board, collect points and get to a distinct and certain end.

This false notion of linearity is apparent when we hear people judge someone who is grieving, "Oh she missed the anger stage," or "He hasn't reached acceptance yet."

I always thought that "losing a loved one" was a euphe-mism used by people who were afraid to say the word dead. But after losing my brother Larry I know that lost is the perfect word to describe the feeling that follows a death.

Though he died several years ago my feeling about my brother is that I have misplaced him; It's that sensation of knowing that my book or that letter I was just reading, are around here somewhere...if I could just remember where I left him. Something just out of reach, still here, but also gone.

I think this is why we can sometimes be so hard on the grieving, and why we want them to go through those stages and be done with it. We love closure and things that are sealed and settled. But death and grief, for all their seeming finality, are not as final as we would like.

So tonight I'll make cocoa and light candles; we'll look at pictures and tell stories and we'll laugh.

The root of the word grieve is heavy. We carry our dead as a cherished burden. Death ends a life, but not a relationship. Who would want to close the door on that?

Shooting From the Hip

When I was in kindergarten my favorite outfit was a red and white cowgirl dress. It had a red twill skirt, a red and white gingham shirt, and a vest that was decorated with white leatherette fringe and a swirl of rhinestone studs. The most important part of this ensemble was my holster with two six-shooters. I remember practicing fancy sharp-shooting like Dale Evans and Roy Rogers did on TV. I loved my guns.

Now looking back, even as I count the rows of shoes and purses in my closet, it's clear that even then my guns were accessories rather than preparation for my second amendment responsibilities.

I thought about my first guns this week when I set out to understand the Second Amendment Sisters. This is the women's organization that was recently formed as a counter protest to the Million-Mom March. The SAS are, according to their materials, gun-owning and gun-loving women. They are also mothers who share the soccer mom's love of kids, home and country.

Well, I did want to understand what they were about. I don't see a problem with the fact that some women like to shoot guns. And I can relate to the vulnerability many women feel. I lived in a high crime city for years and I learned what you need to learn to live in that urban reality.

But feelings about guns and crime are separate from what is at the heart of the dispute between the Million Moms and The Second Amendment Sisters. I got the "Sisters" press releases, visited their website, and perused their recommended books: Armed and Female, and Dial 911 and Die. If we are to believe the sound bites, the "sisters", just like the Million Moms, want their kids and communities to be safe.

It is "how" that is at question. Reducing the total number of guns makes sense to those of us on the soccer mom side, even though we know the bad guys will still have theirs. We depend on law enforcement in that department. The "Sisters" don't trust that process; they are not waiting for the cops. They want their own gun in their own home— or car or purse--and they will defend themselves. That's the point of their book, Dial 911 and Die. It's the screenplay for the worst woman-at-home-alone-the-bad-guys-are-in-the-house nightmare.

But even if that was the real heart of the sisters' concern, I could say they mean well. When I lived alone in rural New York, I felt much more fear than I did in the city. I wondered many a night how well my weapon of choice, a can of hair spray, would defend me. But I made my ultimate decision to not buy a gun based not on a creaking house and too many scary movies, but on recalling the stories of innocent people killed by scared homeowners.

I read the three-page mission statement of the SAS, and after a compelling case for social responsibility and strong parenting, I came to the punch line: "An armed citizenry has proven to be the best deterrent to government abuse." So this isn't about domestic violence, rape, street crime and Columbine after all? No, the real issue here is gun registration and it may be the very Solomon's choice that outs these "Sisters".

It's an easy guess that the NRA have a hand-- and a couple hundred grand-- in the "Sisters" effort. The NRA's official word is, "Oh no, those are just the other Moms." But truth telling isn't a NRA strong suit. There's a story in this week's Nation magazine that describes how the NRA, in a recent California senate race, sent in undercover volunteers to support a Democratic newcomer to oust the Democratic incumbent who favored gun control. But the NRA directed their members, "Do not let on that you are associated with the NRA, keep the hats and sweatshirts at home."

This is what infuriates me about the "Sisters". The NRA hiding behind women's skirts convinces me that this is really a bunch of militia members in drag. And their stand-by-your-militia-man women are playing along.

None of this is about kids or safety. The target of all this emotional ammo is the big showdown in November. When I read the SAS statement that concludes, "Government sponsored safety will always be followed by the heavy hand of oppression," I'm just seeing Charlton Heston in a dress.

The Hidden Casualties of War

At the start of American sporting events we stand up to sing the national anthem. It's a teaching moment. At a high school game a parent snatches a hat from a youngster or glowers at a texting teen, "Get on your feet." And they do.

For many sporting events there is now another requisite moment during the game when we observe a "tribute to our Armed Forces serving overseas." A soldier in full dress, with excellent posture, comes onto the field and for that moment we pause again. We feel virtuous and patriotic.

We mean it—we really do. For anywhere from ten to almost 60 seconds we really care about the men and women of our military. We feel appreciation and even concern. And then satisfied that we have cared, and as the soldier, so beautifully decorated, is escorted out of sight, we return to our debate about favorite teams and best commercials.

Our soldiers are dying. They are dying the way that soldiers have always died—killed in combat and by tragic wartime accidents but they are also—increasingly--dying at home by their own hands. That is the part we don't see, don't honor and don't stand up for.

The soldiers we see at sporting events are clean and composed and they exude strength and will and endurance. The conceit is that they are there to remind us of the hardship they endure for us, but in fact they may be there to cajole us into believing that the respect we feel for them is enough.

What if during the Super Bowl or on Baseball's Opening Day we saw a group of American soldiers twitching with the physical and mental pain of post-combat fatigue, stress and disability? Not the heroic amputee—we know that symbol of sacrifice—but the one whose hope, sanity and peace have been cut off? What if we stood for 60 seconds to witness the grown men and women who serve and protect us while they shake and cry and go numb? What if we saw them as they struggle to manage their depression, anxiety and dissociation?

As our nation's longest war approaches ten years we are approaching a terrifying statistic. The Army's own 2010 briefing on military suicide reported that, "If we include accidental death, which frequently is the result of high-risk behavior (drugs, alcohol, driving) we find that less young men and women die in combat than by their own actions." It is for these men and women that we should be holding our hands over our hearts.

I don't come from a military family. My understanding of this collateral damage came when I spent a few years interviewing China Marines—pre-World War II veterans. In China they experienced the combination of bloody atrocity and deadly boredom that today's soldiers endure. The men I visited were in their 80's when they told me how they still—65 years later—struggled with their addictions, insomnia, grief, and tragically, how their trauma had impacted their families –some for two generations.

We are slow learners. Military mental illness is always with us. It's had many names –all euphemisms to keep it just out of sight. It is War Fatigue, Shell Shock, Viet Nam Syndrome and Post-Traumatic Stress Disorder.

Every faith has a tenet that asks us not to close our eyes to suffering. And here too we should not look away. This is not to say that war is wrong, but we should know what it really means when we stand to say it's worth it.

Getting Ready for Thanksgiving

Even though it's been years since I had Thanksgiving with my own family I still get nervous as this holiday approaches. When I was growing up, November always brought a wave of panic. My mother wanted the house to be nicer than it was, so each year we were subjected to a frenzy of last-minute decorating on a shoestring.

One year she bought cases of caulking compound to remedy the drafty chill. We had that caulking goop for years and in the summer we used the guns to play Combat. Another year she decided to make over the master bedroom. Her plan was to "tent" the bed in yards of gauzy fabric. But my mother didn't know how to sew; she could picture the end result but not how to get there. We had that fabric for years. I made togas for Latin class, we wrapped gifts in it, and ten years later, when my niece got married, we made shower decorations with the last of our pastel yard goods.

While my mother was decorating, my father cooked. He would stay up all night tending the bird. On Thanksgiving morning the scent of baking pies was added to the aroma of roasting turkey, and that would combine with the odors of Spic & Span and dusting spray, as my mother furiously cleaned.

Tension ran high. We were shouted into baths and clean clothes. When the doorbell rang at noon, we smelled and looked good.

Aunt Junie always arrived first and brought her own pies. Yes, she knew my father was making the dessert--he did every year--but every year she brought her own pies and acted surprised. What can I say? She was his older sister. Sibling stuff doesn't age out, it just gets played out in new ways.

Next was Aunt Martha, who pinched us –hard –on the cheek. We'd whine to our mother, and be told, "Be nice to her, she doesn't have any children," as if that explained why she wanted to torture someone else's. Then there was Uncle Elmer who had one eye that drifted to the side and a big warty growth on his cheek. We perfected air kissing to deal with holiday hellos.

Soon the house would be filled with people. The cousins went straight to chasing and teasing each other. We saw then, but only knew later, the significance of each cousin's ways: The one who always stood back to watch is now the writer; the cousin who schmoozed with the adults became a politician, and the one who happily ran to get refills for the grown-ups--finishing off their drinks enroute—is now a popular speaker on the recovery circuit.

Of course we didn't see the adult side of things. I didn't know about the barbs my mother got about our old house from the Aunt who "married better." I didn't know that this pain was the fuel to my mother's annual decorating frenzy. I also didn't know until later that the men sitting around the kitchen table were zinging their own darts at my Dad. He was the only one who had finished school and moved "upstairs" in the plant. Now I see why he had to excuse himself so often to "check on the turkey."

Most of our families have a version of these scenes. On Thanksgiving we'll be humming, "We gather together….", but mothers will sigh over daughter's hair, the childless will offer parenting advice, and the uncle who has plenty will tell those who have none how they should invest their money. Old wounds will be given a good jab, intentionally or not.

We come to this meal each year hoping for the holiday we remember from childhood, the one with laughter and fun. So if the tension rises in your dining room this Thanksgiving, just consider it a warm-up for the December holidays to come, and like a warning shot fired over our feelings, let's remember to be gentle with and grateful for the people we sit down with.

The Office Holiday Party

We are entering the time of year that makes seasoned managers cringe and human resource directors want to leave town. Fine words to the contrary, there is little Peace on Earth at the office now: It's time for the office Christmas, oops, I mean "holiday" party. Yes, we've learned to choke on the word Christmas and insist that the December party where we dress in sparkles, bring wrapped gifts and drink eggnog standing next to an evergreen tree is just a winter event. But language games are the least of it when management has to plan the annual—"no one will be happy no matter what we do"--office holiday party.

This time of year career gurus remind us: you must attend, you should not drink, don't dress like a stripper and do make small talk with many people. The warnings should certainly be heeded. The annual holiday party is ground zero for what is known in Human Resources as the CLM, or Career Limiting Move. CLM's include Xeroxing body parts, getting tanked with co-workers and making jokes about the boss to his/her spouse. But love them --or leave them early-- the office holiday party is a ritual of the workplace.

The list of issues is long: do we go out on the town or stay in the building? Is the event during work or after hours? Will there be dancing? Music? And biggest bugaboo: booze or no booze? Divisiveness is in the details. One of the words tossed around liberally in the weeks leading up to the party is "they" as in they don't have kids, they don't like to drink, they drink too much, or they don't have to pay a baby-sitter. Preferences also break down by personality type: Extroverts love the parties; Introverts want to die.

Some offices give money to charity instead but then end up bringing in a deli tray on December 22nd because it doesn't feel right not to do something. I think it hits us that if we don't have some kind of party, then we're admitting that this is work and that these people are not really our family or our best friends. It's one of the passive deceptions we engage in to smooth life along.

So what's at the heart of this holiday ritual? Well, for starters we have strong cultural memories and it's dark this time of year and we are longing for light. Workplaces have their own kind of darkness, so it's human to want to brighten that up too.

But there's more. The office party is really a throwback. Yes, that sushi with sparkles affair in the boardroom is a remnant from the Ebenezer Scrooge days. It's a flashback to the days when Big Daddy Corporation rewarded its child-like workers with a decent meal and glass of bubbly they could not provide for themselves. The company party was also a time to reset any drifting notions of who owned the means of production.

I remember that kind of event. At the box factory where my Dad worked, the assembly line was shut down once a year: the Saturday before Christmas. Hot dogs were served from the corrugator and Santa arrived on a forklift. There were no Bring Your Kids to Work days back then, so the Christmas Party was the chance to see where Dad went to work every day. It was simply understood that the family depended on this place and these people.

As our economy takes a turn, we may have come full circle. So step up to the Holiday Office Event: Put on your sparkles, exclaim over the deli tray, and admit to your peers that you couldn't have done it without them. They will remember that gift all year.

Aging Parents

I write sitting at the table of a summer house in the middle of winter. We are here in Canada now because Peter's mother is in the hospital—again. Each time her stay is longer, each time her breathing more labored, and each time the doctor's concern more pointed. We come to help, advise, persuade and finally to make the decisions for her.

It's an uncomfortable process taking over our parent's lives. First it was the car keys, then her checkbook, even the teakettle had to go, boiled dry one time too many.

There is comfort in numbers. The group of Americans caring for elderly parents is a growing crowd. Seven of us turn age 50 every minute, with folks who live longer and with more needs. AARP reports that an estimated 22.5 million households –that's one in four—provide care for someone over 60, while according to the National Center for Health Statistics, life expectancy has risen from 69 years in 1960 to 78 years in 1998. We have met the elderly and they are us—and ours. The generation that didn't trust anyone over 30 is now over 50 and caring for folks over 70.

We in this "sandwich generation," squeezed between the demands of children, parents, spouses and careers are sitting at the kitchen table writing one check for tuition and another for extended care.

But it's not just the money. This uncomfortable role of being the big cheese for the family raises new questions and unspoken worries about care and responsibility.

It used to be that there was a pause in midlife between getting your kids out of the house and moving your folks in; a pause that meant adult contemplation and time to face one's own mortality, a time to focus and re-group for part II: life after midlife.

Past generations watched their parents die and learned what they wanted and needed from that close look at mortality and then –ideally—made better choices about how to live their own later years. Now we face two retirements at the same time, planning retirement from our work while retiring our role of being child of our parent. Because these tasks are now compressed, we lose that insight and that breather between life stages. For many it's simply tiring.

Many of us commiserate with colleagues and maybe let close friends hear the ambivalence —the fear and guilt we feel about our parents--but there's another group we need to include in this care and conversation: our own kids.

The next generation needs to be in on how we are with our parents, not just because we need a hand, but also to wise them up about their future with us. We'll be living a lot longer, too, and our generation, with its sense of empowerment and self-sufficiency, won't be going off to nursing care any easier than those in their 70s and 80s today.

We need to let the next generation see our ambivalence, not to spare them from it—we can't—but to offer the understanding that the pain that comes with this territory is built in and that their own future reluctance and resistance will be normal. Give them permission now to take our car keys and the checkbook and yes, even the teakettle, when that time comes.

We live this circle: breaking away from parents, becoming parents, taking on our own parents and then allowing our kids to parent us. Just as we had to back away from the ones we raised as they became young adults, we now reverse the process and intrude into our parents' lives and choices.

We need to let our younger family know how this works and how this feels. We need to give them fair warning and a bit of a break. Say to them, "Look closely, some day this task will be yours; someday this dance will be you and me".

Counting Down February's Cold

I wake in the night and listen. The reassuring rumble tells me that the furnace is still on. It's good news and bad. It means we have heat and there's still oil, but at this hour I visualize the dollar bills that might just as well be fuel.

I don't fall back to sleep easily. A glass of water and check on the dogs, curled like Danish pastries on their pillows; I'm awake and afraid in the cold night.

My fear of cold has an ancient echo. I listen for the furnace at night the way my Polish ancestors woke in their huts to check on the fire.

With only 28 days, February is the longest month, and we secretly count it down. February is to winter what Wednesday is to the workweek: If we can get through February, even snow in April won't rock us.

In many wedding albums there is a picture of the groom carrying the bride over the threshold. That odd custom is also about staying warm. In ancient times when a woman left her father's home and was set down on the hearth in her new house, she was in the most important spot in any ancient home. She literally kept the home fires burning.

Temperature is part of my own married romance. Coming to New York from Baltimore –where there is just one decent snowstorm each year--I too was set down on a new hearth. I married Peter, who comes from Northern Ontario where winter runs from September to May and wind chill is scoffed at. "When Canadians have 30 below, they mean it, he says; "Wind chill is for wimps".

So to marry this tundra man I had to learn to dress for cold. To get me from the Inner Harbor to the frozen Hudson, Peter plied me with jackets and sweaters, scarves and gloves, even a hat with earflaps. His gift of Sorel boots toasty at Canada's 30 below, was a sign we were getting serious.

But physical acclimation is real. That first winter, living in upstate New York, I thought I'd die. My boots were good below freezing, but my fingers could barely tie them. Each year it gets easier. Now I complain about the cold, but no longer imagine myself part of the Donner party.

But there is also an emotional acclimation to cold. A quote from Camus is taped inside the cabinet where I get my coffee mug each morning. It says: "In the depth of winter, I finally learned that within me there lay an invincible summer." Some days that tells me that I have enough beach memories to cling to on the slippery slope of February, and other days it is the word "invincible" that reminds me that living cold does indeed build character.

But having a warm house is important. I can't swear that my first marriage ended solely over the thermostat setting, but for years I never went on a second date with a man whose response to my "I'm cold," was "Put on a sweater." Now I'm happily married to a man who knows that cold hands do not mean a warm heart, and that a big oil bill is better than roses. But surprisingly, I've grown some too. I am willing, in this new life and climate, to go and put on that cost-saving sweater.

The word comfortable did not originally refer to being contented. It's Latin root, confortare, means to strengthen. Hence its use in theology: the Holy Spirit is Comforter; not to make us comfy, but to make us strong. This then is February's task. We may not be warm but we are indeed comforted; we are strong and we are counting the days.

Labor Day Music

If you sit quietly this morning you'll hear a distant bell beginning to sound. That soft warning is coming from inside you. It signals the end of summer and reminds us that on Tuesday we return to our lives in earnest. It's bittersweet, because for the most part, we have good lives and yet there was all that hope and good intention a dozen weeks ago. It is always only partly realized by Labor Day.

If there was a sound track for this weekend it would be composed of the sad but inspiring music of America's Labor Movement.

America has a rich tradition of labor songs. These anthems are songs of suffering, determination and desire. This music echoes deep in the American bloodstream because most of us, regardless of our current station, come from families that once worked that hard, that physically and with that kind of hope for better lives. Many of us have realized the lives that our predecessors worked and organized for. The music still moves us because working songs contain our hopes and hurts, our angers, fears and aspirations.

Listening to labor music we can hear the entire history of American industry. Whether it's "Hard Times in the Mill" about how Cotton boys don't make enough/To buy them tobacco and a box of snuff, or "A Miner's Life" with it's warning of both natural dangers (Watch the rocks, they're falling daily), and exploitation, (Keep your hand upon the dollar and your eye upon the scale.)

Working people have used music to protest their conditions, to celebrate heroes and to rally one another. While most labor songwriters are unknown, there are many who deserve recognition. One is Florence Reece. On the night a band of deputies broke into her home to arrest her husband Sam, a union organizer, she tore a page from the wall calendar and wrote what may be one of the most demanding and defiant songs of coal workers: "Which Side Are You On?"

Woody Guthrie, of "This Land is Your Land," fame is perhaps the most recognized balladeer of working-class life. Songs like "So Long, It's Been Good to Know You" (on the migrants of the Great Depression) and "Union Maid" (praising the courage of union women) can be read as chapters in American Labor history.

Many of the best labor songs were written by a Swedish immigrant named Joe Hill. Hill worked as a harvester, a miner and a seaman, and he was committed to radical trade unionism. He organized workers who were being exploited but who had been ignored by the American Federation of Labor. His songs fanned the flames of discontent among unskilled immigrants, itinerant workers and racially excluded Blacks, Mexicans and Asians. Hill's career was cut short when he was executed in Utah in 1915 on what historians agree were trumped up murder charges. He is remembered for his parting words to union leader Bill Haywood, "Don't mourn. Organize." Even more memorable are the 1938 lyrics of another labor songwriter, Earle Robinson:

I dreamed I saw Joe Hill last night,
alive as you and me.
Says I, "But Joe, you're ten years dead."
"I never died," says he,
"I never died", says he.

Joe Hill will live as long as there are people whose working conditions are not right. Most of us have safe places to work, decent pay and hours that allow us to have lives and families outside of work. This is not true for all workers in our country and certainly not true for the people around the world who make the clothes and gadgets and the lovely goods we depend on for our way of life.

So perhaps while we fight traffic and shoppers this weekend, we might also sing along with some gratitude for those who picked, plucked, hacked, drilled, dug-- and fought-- for our enviable working lives.

Father's Day Time

One of the central attractions in the city of Prague is the clock tower in the main square. There is a certain irony that vacationers, supposedly freed from clock watching, are drawn to this tower clock. They arrive five minutes before each hour to stare upward at the moving hands and the parade of carved wooden puppets that mark each changing hour. Tours guides offer stern warnings that the area near the tower is notorious for petty crime. While tourists are transfixed by the clock and its puppets, pickpockets help themselves to money, passports and yes, watches.

The tradition of village clock towers evolved from the practice of having a man stand guard to keep watch and periodically ring a bell to mark the hour. The name of that profession is the origin of the watch we now wear on our wrist. Timepieces gradually moved from the public clocks of the middle ages, to clocks inside the home, to pocket watches, to ones now strapped on our arm, getting closer to us all the time. While convenience has advantages, we no longer enjoy the communal reminder of passing time.

Time is an important topic for Father's Day. This week's newspaper ads show this deep connection. From Timex to Rolex, wristwatches are the number one gift for Dad. It may be the perfect gift too. Fatherhood is a short season and it flies by.

My father died when he was 56 and I was 18. His death was sudden and unexpected. It wasn't until I crossed the 50 threshold that I understood that my father had died young. I knew, of course, that I was young when he died, but now I know that he was young too. Age, like time, is relative.

Time was an important part of my father's life. He was an industrial engineer, a "time and motion study man." His work was about efficiency and calculation. He carried a clipboard and wore an elegant gold Hamilton watch.

Whether due to nature or nurture, I too have an overly developed sense of time. I multi-task, write daily to-do lists, and I lust after organizing systems. But I also resist being tethered to time. Maybe it's because I watched my father save so much time, which he never got a chance to use, that I have a love/hate relationship with "time management."

My own calendar shocks people. It's an oversized month-at-a-glance book in which I track tasks by scribbling through the borders and across the lines intended to demarcate the days. Each month's page becomes an abstract work of scribbles and swirls and then it's torn away. I don't look back.

Death isn't the only way that dads go missing from their kids' lives. Divorce or drinking can do it too, but most often it's work. That's not new. Fathers of the 1950s didn't come to school plays or Girl Scout ceremonies; Mom came and told Dad about it at dinner.

Are today's Dads wiser? It seems so. Last year fathers reported spending four hours a day with their kids, compared with just 2.7 hours in 1965. But I wonder, are those hours together real leisure and pleasure or are we multitasking the homework and the errands with the quality time? It's a cliché to say how fast childhood goes and how fast fatherhood disappears too, but it's true.

With our lists and calendars-- and even our watches—
we can pick our own pockets. In trying to better organize
them our lives can be stolen away.
Next week summer begins. Will the livin' be easy? Or
will we tick it off and time it out? Fathers, keep watch.
Just look at the time.

Spiritual Materialism

We're in the countdown to Christmas with just seven days to go. Some of us are dashing to the mall; some are glued to the Internet, hoping that the promise of "delivery before Christmas" is true, and others are clutching copies of "The One Hundred Dollar Christmas" and smugly announcing that they are "Just not into the gift thing" this year.

It's begun to seem that there is a chic, anti-chic in some circles making it de rigueur to disdain shopping and to bemoan the consumerism that has overtaken this holiday.

While I have certainly bashed the rise of the consumer culture, I'm now wondering if it's also possible for some people to enjoy austerity a tad too much? Yes, I am guilty of laughing at "Jungle Bell Rock Santa" dolls and of rolling my eyes at holiday décor that has too many plastic figurines. But I'm rethinking. I mean, where's the fun in all white lights and no tinsel?

While I know that simplifying our lives is a good thing, I also experience annoyance with those who are so disdainful of shoppers, especially when these non-shoppers need to cast their choice as somehow spiritually superior. It's just too easy to point at someone with a bag full of brand name goods and label it superficial, but isn't it possible that spiritual asceticism can be just as shallow?

Consumerism is based on the belief that all problems have a material solution. We recognize it in the race to bigger houses, fancier cars and the need for the latest techno gadgets. But for some people spiritual practices or even religion can be used the same way, as just another "product" to fix one's life.

One of the places we see this is in spiritual consumerism—when we keep the value of consumption but dress it up in higher-minded garb. One of the ways that this form of consumerism plays out is in the impulse to collect spiritual experiences: things like going on retreats and pilgrimages or studying with the best-selling teachers or the coolest guru. We become a spiritual tourist, not unlike someone who has to visit all the national parks, but who drives through each one, checks it off his list and brings home postcards and souvenirs.

By now we all know that many people use consumption as a way to build their ego; they try to change who they are by buying things to fit the image they desire. Count me in; we all do this to some degree. But what we miss is that it's equally flawed to create a self-image based on refusing to participate in the dominant culture or by disdaining those who do. The fundamental error is the same: It's about trying to be special. Whether we derive our identity from consuming or from not consuming we're still focused on our self.

This is one of those paradoxes: Just when you start to feel superior for living a spiritual life, you realize you've slipped out of the spiritual ground. It's kind of like humility: just when you think you've got it, you don't.

Besides, how can thinking we're better than someone else be of any benefit? A line from Wordsworth comes to mind: "Getting and spending we lay waste our powers." But it's also true that in judging and criticizing we waste our lives.

So we're entering a week that takes us straight to the intersection of spirituality and consumption. Can we be kind to our fellows whether they're shopping or not? Can we choose peace in our hearts and at the mall?

The best strategy may be humor. We've just got to laugh a lot this week, and especially at ourselves. Jingle Bell Santa can be our guru. After all, his mantra is, "Ho Ho Ho."

Don't Worry Be Happy

Last week I walked across the street to look through piles of phonograph records and bins of old dishes spread across our neighbor's lawn. Their grown children were cleaning out the house and having a sale. Just weeks before, we'd taken our own boxes of similar things to the thrift store and felt well pleased to have those odds and ends gone. Now we were looking through someone else's stuff, and delighting in finding a "very useful" mixing bowl, and some "these could be handy" small wooden shelves.

The things that most often find their way back to our house are books, and I found myself sitting on the neighbor's porch sifting through boxes of hardbacks and paperbacks. There were the usual yard sale staples: mysteries and romances and a big pile of Reader's Digest Condensed Books. I have a fondness for those; I grew up with them and met many great authors in those striped, four-in-one hardbacks.

In my neighbor's stash was something more I recognized from childhood: a set of books by Dale Carnegie, the grand master of personal improvement. I spotted a copy of his famous How to Make Friends and Influence People, but the book that I reached for was How to Stop Worrying and Start Living. I asked a nearby teenager, "How much?" "Ten cents," said the young gal. I gave her a quarter and walked back to my porch to read the familiar text.

When I was a kid, Dale Carnegie's books were on the top shelf of my father's bookshelf. As a quintessential first-generation, self-improving, education-valuing, always striv-

ing Depression survivor, my father read these books over and
over. And, like the typical second-generation, take-achieve-
ment-for-granted, life-is-easier kids we were, my brothers
and I made fun of Dale Carnegie every chance we got.

I have to tell on myself now, though. I am my father's
daughter. His drive for self-improvement and habit of worry
passed to me by nature or nurture. Over the years I've spent
thousands on classes, courses, workshops and retreats. I've
tried every remedy and herb that promises peace. I even gave
a huge wad of cash and an armload of flowers to get a secret
mantra from Transcendental Meditation.

Now I laugh. I could have just looked at my father's
books. Opening How to Stop Worrying, I skim the table
of contents. The message—in stories and quotes-- is this:
Change your thinking. Change your mind. Be in this day.
Dale Carnegie seemed to know what the Beatles learned
in India: Just let it be. I flipped to the title page and see
that "Worry" was written in 1950, and my copy is from
the 46th printing.

If Dale Carnegie wrote this today he'd be a guru and
superstar; Oprah would have him on her show and he'd do
the celebrity workshop circuit. I grin to imagine that he'd be
rumored to be the man that changed Madonna's life. She'd
wear a gold "DC" necklace instead of a red string, and,
when pushed, she'd whine that no one really understood her
devotion to Dale.

Though he was successful in his day, Dale Carnegie
wrote his books for the post-WWII, GI Bill, self-improving,
house-buying, ladder-of-success fathers of the fifties. His was
a male message since it was presumed that the man of the
house was the one worrying about the bills and the bosses
and how to pay for the babies. That too was my Dad.

My father is not around to thank today. He died before I started my own journey of self-improvement. So I'll claim this musty book as a gift from my father's spirit. There is nothing new under the sun. Be here now; live in this day; laugh at yourself and grow up.

Fashion Shopping Secrets

It's quiz time: Have you ever come home from shopping and left your purchases in the car until you could sneak them into the house? Have you ever pretended a new garment was something you had for ages? Have you ever lied about a price or pretended that a new purchase was on sale? I speak from no moral mountaintop. I was once married to a man with severe color blindness. He thought I had a small wardrobe, mostly brown.

We need to talk about this because now that fall has officially begun, we start to look deep in our closets and find, amidst the boxes and rows and shelves of clothes, that we have nothing to wear. It drives us to the mall.

They say that appearances can be deceiving and they tell us, don't judge a book by its cover, but that same "they" also tell us that we make decisions about others—and they of us—in the first three seconds. That would seem to support an investment in book covers and clothing and managing our appearances.

I am haunted by a remark made years ago. I was working in a downtown office and returned from lunch that day with shopping bags. A co-worker casually inquired where I had been and the receptionist, annoying but prescient, responded, "She's shopping for the life she'll never live." We laughed, but I was stunned that his remark cut so deeply and so quickly to the heart of the matter, to the heart of me.

We use clothes, and therefore shop, to try on-- and try out --new selves. We practice our life or the lives we think we might like. We are told, and we believe, that we can dress for success and that clothing will empower us, but does clothing illustrate our life, enhance it? Or consume it? A line from a Wordsworth poem echoes: "Getting and spending we lay waste our powers."

Advertising alone can't explain why we shop again and again. And there's more to dressing ourselves than trying to look nice or be comfortable or to attract erotic attention. Clothes proclaim –and disguise—our identity. And, as with speaking or writing or other forms of expression, some of us are more eloquent, while others are inclined to stutter, stiffen or confuse their messages.

Last year Yves St. Laurent said that it was time for him to retire "because fashion has changed." It's a funny statement about an industry that is all about reinvention and changing wardrobes. It goes to show that superficiality can be very deep.

What do women want? Freud asked that. And the truest answer is: A really, really good black skirt; shoes that go from office to evening; and a trench coat that makes one look both smart and sexy.

But kidding aside--except for the skirt--what do we want? Here's what I think: We want affiliation, love, real friendships, self-esteem, work that uses the best of us, and genuine leisure—not just a swapping of to-do lists from weekday to week-end.

If we get just a few of these in one lifetime we're doing well. But we're Americans, we've been to therapy and we read books; we want those other things too.

This is our vulnerability. Those intangible and constant needs get linked to goods—dresses, shoes, suits. So we go back again and again to the mall, the discount store or the designer boutique to get a fix.

It almost works, but because our souls aren't sated by style, we're hungry again.

But look in the closet; how many lives can one person live? Politics may be backsliding, but fashion forges ahead. Where will it take us this year? Can we dress for the life we are living and not waste another minute?

God Goes to Work

Inside my day planner I have written these words: Laborare est Orare. It's the motto of the Benedictine Order of Monks and it translates: Work is Prayer. But I hadn't thought, until recently, about how many people are actually praying at work.

It's not uncommon to hear a co-worker say something like, "Pray that delivery gets there on time" or "I hope to God this deal works out," but most of us don't suspect the number of colleagues who go to their offices and literally "hope to God".

The June 9th issue of Fortune magazine has a cover story called "God and Business" about people who bring their Sunday values into their Monday world, and, according to Fortune, there are a lot of prayers rising up from office buildings all over America.

What is our reaction when we think that someone might actually be praying on the job? Do we roll our eyes? Feel a sense of quaint embarrassment? Ask to join in? If we consider that more than 90% of Americans say they believe in God, and 89% say they pray every day, it makes sense that some of that prayer would be in the office.

But you're not alone if that makes you uneasy, because it's not a simple thing when God comes to work. Diversity training has taught us that best practice means not trying to whitewash the workplace or removing all symbols of culture and belief but allowing differences to be celebrated and respected. The hard part is that when God goes to work, He or She often brings not just the New Age rainbow raiment of acceptance but very often the strident symbols of specific religions and cultures. Even with the best intentions warm and fuzzy spirituality can get poked by the sharp edges of organized religion.

It raises a lot of questions that may not have satisfactory answers. Federal law requires "reasonable accommodation" of religious practices in the workplace. But the trouble is that there are often inherent conflicts. I have a friend who works with a man, a senior manager in her company, and she wonders if she's right to worry that his particular religion could get in the way of promoting women. Another friend tells of major conflicts at her company where the deeply religious HR director advocated for a health plan that did not cover contraception.

But walk through the office again and look at office bookshelves or take a peek in your co-worker's briefcase and you'll see books with titles like "God at Work," "Jesus, Inc." or "What Would Buddha do at Work." These are just a few of the new offerings from the fastest growing segment of the publishing industry. The "Inspirational," and more specifically, "Faith at Work" segments of publishing have grown 31 percent in the last four years. According to Publishers Weekly, the industry trade journal, we're spending more than $900 million on these books each year.

Clearly we're looking for some kind of help that the Employee Assistance Program isn't offering. We want faith in something to get us through the week, and we want to know how to reconcile the prophets and the profits. But it may also be that we're taking old values and giving them a new spin.

When I read the individual profiles in the Fortune article, I was a little dismayed. I had expected to learn how business people who were "out" as believers struggled with the legal and political aspects of their faith, but instead the stories were of people who are, well, simply good people: decent, honest and caring. What struck me was that they sounded kind of old fashioned until I realized that what they had was what we used to call good character.

It looks to me like we've discovered some value in our parents' values after all. But true to form, we're now dressing up stodgy old "good character" in the hipper garb of being spiritual at work.

Rationing Healthcare

A century ago George Bernard Shaw wrote a play called "The Doctor's Dilemma" that presaged one of the central issues of our current healthcare crisis. In the play a doctor must decide whether to use the last dose of a tuberculosis vaccine to save an aging fellow physician or a young artist. The play is a conversation about the value of life and who decides who lives or dies. Without ever using the word, Shaw's play touches on rationing, a key topic in our current healthcare debate.

To talk about rationing or its euphemism "allocation" effectively, we have to cut through the rhetoric and stop being so ethically prissy. We'd like to pretend that rationing is something insurance companies cooked up, but the truth is we've been rationing healthcare for ages, and we're all party to that plan.

In Medicaid and Medicare there are payment caps and a long list of services not covered. Rationing. In general medicine there are "standards of care" that determine when a specimen is taken or a procedure used. Rationing. Some of us have HMO plans that come with a physician referral process, and long waits for appointments. Rationing. Even the few of us who have indemnity plans, what we call "good health insurance," have to deal with provider panels and mandatory second opinions. Rationing.

Rationing is uncomfortable to talk about. The new gene therapy may work for cancer, but should it always be used and for everyone? Is it granny killing to deny chemotherapy to an 80-year-old who has Alzheimer's? And what about organ transplants? Yes, if you are 27, but no if you are 72? And what about the highly emotional area of pediatric care? We talk about the use of extraordinary measures, but the ground keeps moving. Today's basic medical protocols were yesterday's extraordinary measures. We can't bring ourselves to admit it but if we provide all premature babies with expensive care, and prolong the lives of all of the elderly, while also trying to meet the demands of boomers who have little tolerance for normal aging, we'll run out.

One reason we cannot properly frame this conversation is our reluctance to talk about a fact even more challenging than the need for rationing. The most uncomfortable topic that is buried in the center of our healthcare conversation is the reality of death.

We are scared that there won't be enough transplants, gene therapy or expensive treatments and someone might have to die. Our distaste for rationing is actually our fear of the bigger fact that life itself is rationed. We still think death is preventable. Here's the real bottom-line: We don't get out of here alive.

Illness, disease and death are not necessarily things that shouldn't happen. Look down: you live in a human body. It will break down, misfire and die. That's not an accident or a mistake.

We distort our language and our thinking to hide this from ourselves. We talk about a cure for cancer as a way to save lives, but what a cure for cancer will do is save deaths from cancer. Then you get to die from something else. We are so uncomfortable with death that we can't think clearly.

To remedy this we need to bring different players to the table. We need the big thinkers: philosophers, bio-ethicists, linguists and historians.

We also need members of the faith communities. Life and death, and distributive justice are their business.

As much as we want to respect life, we also need to honor death. Then we can talk rationally about healthcare.

Love After Valentine's Day

Last week we honored love. We wore red, ate chocolate, sent cards and laughed. This week the candy is gone, flowers faded, Valentine cards tucked in a drawer, and perhaps we've gotten mad or shed some tears.

In popular culture love is always in the news--love gained and love lost.

Two new books on the bestseller list are about both. Elizabeth Gilbert's "Committed" and "Marriage and Other Acts of Charity" by Kate Braestrup. Both of these are second books about second marriage –love gained--for authors whose first books described love lost. One remarried after divorce, the other after a death.

For several years I've taught a writing class for 10th grade boys and girls. One of the exercises we do is making a list of people in the news and connecting them to a work of art. For the past five years Jen and Angelina and Brad have topped the list when kids are asked, "Who's in the news?" We're fascinated. (Yes, you too, don't pretend. It's pure demographics and dollars. They are on the cover of those magazines because their story interests --and sells. If we cared about poets, Anne Carson would be on the cover of People.)

Jen and Brad and Angelina stay in the headlines of celebrity news because this trio is our perfect triangle: The Good Girl, the Bad Girl and the Boy. Saint Valentine was a Roman, but our fascination with the triumvirate of love gone bad is pure Greek. We crave the stark black-and-white split: Evil Woman and Saintly Victim. And yes, the naïve, benign Him.

We need these "gods" to act out our beliefs and fears—conscious or not. Jen, Brad and Angelina work hard for us. They play out in exaggerated form the dilemmas and complexities of us mortals. What do Good Jen and Bad Angelina do for us? They help us hold our treasured dichotomy. Otherwise we'd have to look in the mirror. No marriage ever ended because of one person. But to face that, we'd have to live in the gray of humanity. And because we hurt when love is lost, we blame. And so our "gods" act out the crime and punishment.

What is wonderfully human is that even when love is lost, we keep believing in it and in the triumph of hope over experience. No one—even in the worst marriage --didn't think at sometime "We are the exception; we'll beat the odds." And tough odds they are for Americans: 50% of marriages end in divorce. —So why do it? Perhaps because the more compelling statistic is this: 100% of all marriages end.

Last weekend for Valentine's Day there were many proposals, many weddings. We celebrate those beginnings. But what if we have it backwards? What if we've ignored a crucial element in new love? We're forgetting that every beginning- first date, proposal or wedding- is the result of—and could not exist without—an ending. We need all of the no's and all of the broken hearts to get to a yes. It's true that we prefer that the no's be experienced by someone else, but what adult has had a "yes" –in any part of their life--not preceded by a "no"? If we'll have love, we'll have both no and yes.

Maybe now, a week after Valentine's Day, we could have a holiday to honor love that's ended. We'll go down trying. Even knowing that either divorce or death will end every marriage, we can still believe in loving and in being loved.

The Mary Month of May

I grew up in a Protestant family. My brothers and I went to Sunday school, got confirmed, and later married in the same Methodist Church on Pittsburgh's North side. Overall, it was a good experience. But I always envied Catholic girls, especially in May.

Our working class neighborhood was a mixture of Protestant and Catholic families. Kids were divided by schools: Spring Hill Public or Saint Ambrose Catholic. But it was a close neighborhood and we all played together after school. One mother could stand in for another when it came to discipline or first aid. The differences were few, but to me the Catholic girls seemed to have something special.

In second grade my real feelings of envy emerged. My Catholic friends were having their First Holy Communion. The Protestant church had nothing like it. My friends got to wear poofy white dresses and headbands with flowers and little veils. They were given medals with pictures of saints on them and, most intriguing, they got scapulars.

A scapular consists of two small patches of cloth with holy pictures on them, connected by a long loop of string. I saw friends' scapulars when we went swimming, and they told me that it protected them from the devil and all manner of evil. The Catholic girls wore them tucked inside their sleeveless cotton undershirts, and it was a sin, they told me, to take it off. The idea of a passionate commitment to something, even a string with holy pictures, was very appealing.

As we grew, Catholicism offered my friends other comforts. As a kid I would have liked a patron saint or a guardian angel, but the Methodist church didn't offer those. Now this was at the same age that I was fascinated with writing in code, creating invisible ink, becoming a blood sister, playing with the Ouija board and making up secret societies. I made myth and magic out of anything I could get my hands and mind around.

I think the best thing, though, that Catholic girls got was Mary. She was presented as motherhood and obedience and sweetness, but Catholic girls got a very clear message that there was a woman in heaven, that somebody understood the female side of things.

For Protestant girls, Mary shows up once a year-- at Christmas --to give birth. She might get mentioned on Good Friday—but only in the background. No role model, no intercessor, no friend.

My Catholic pals had statues of Mary. Some had plastic glow-in-the-dark Mary statues, and the older girls had painted plaster Marys, with blue robes and big doe eyes like my Barbie. And Mary was always standing on a snake. I certainly did not understand the symbolism, but it was clear to me at age ten that this 12-inch woman had some power you could not buy for Barbie.

Best of all, my friends had May altars. A May altar was basically a small table with an old lace tablecloth thrown over it. They put their Mary statues on it and had flowers and candles that they were allowed to light when they said their prayers.

Catholic girls had total permission to identify with the feminine in spiritual matters. But no one gave little Protestant girls such romantic, mysterious things to do or own.

This carried over into all of a Catholic girl's life. Mary got prayers, devotions, pilgrimages and even architectural consideration: there is a Marian shrine in every Catholic church. Talk about having a room of one's own. Mary's presence meant that the Catholic Church included at least one woman at a high level. In her assumption into heaven, Mary had broken Christianity's glass ceiling.

We pretty much get the shape of our beliefs early on, and what Catholic girls got was a She and a Her, someone like them, to pray to. And they got all those accessories: medals, scapulars, rosaries, ruffled altar skirts and little white prayer books. Protestant girls got black leatherette New Testaments, Jesus stories, but nothing that said, "We're glad you're a girl."

Of course, later Catholic girls ran into the birth control issue and the limits on their role in the church, but what I saw my Catholic girl friends get was faith in their girlhood and an image of feminine power. It's not a bad way to start out.

No Problem

When parents or teachers are beginning to train young children in the ways of being social, we often begin with simple exchanges. We teach them to say hello and good-bye. Then, with even very young children, we begin to encourage them to recognize and express appreciation or gratitude to those around them.

When we are teaching manners—the code word for this civilizing necessity—we typically model for children what to say. When they are given a gift or a compliment, we say to them, "Say thank you to Aunt Mary" and the child parrots back a rote, "Thank you, Aunt Mary." After some repetitions of this we move to the simple prompt, "What do you say?" and gradually the child learns to say, "Thank you," connecting those words to the context until it becomes second nature to follow a gift or a kind gesture with thanks.

Alas, while that practice continues, and is part of what makes raising small humans so tedious and so rewarding, we have failed in what comes next. So focused have we become on teaching gratitude and thanks that we neglect to note that it is part of a social form, or ritual, if you will, that includes a response on the part of the first person.

Yes, what do you say after someone says thank you to you? The ritualized response is, "You're welcome." So how, oh how, did we get from "Thank you" and "You're welcome" to "No problem"?

"No problem" is a non sequitur—that word from the Latin meaning, "it does not follow"—suggesting that language should follow a sequenced response. (In a marriage like mine where both parties have some small hearing loss, non-sequiturs are frequent and often funny: Him: "Do you think it will rain?" Me: "No, I'd rather fly."

Yes, we most often hear "No problem" from younger people and perhaps this strange locution comes from rejection of social forms. Perhaps "No problem" is a refusal of gratitude on a larger cultural scale, or perhaps it arises from a generation of T-Ball players who each received their own trophy --win or lose-- because everyone's faux self-esteem was at risk?

Fussing over "No problem" versus "You're welcome" may seem a petty complaint. I assure you, it's not. Imagine that you are the one who is helping or giving, that you're a waiter, a salesperson or a teacher. You've done or said something nice—you did a task well or you were kind and the recipient says, "Thank you." They have acknowledged that you were good or nice or talented etc. The traditional response to their thanks, "You're welcome," is a way to say, "Thanks for noticing that," and "Yes, it was my intention to be helpful and I'm glad I was." The words "You're welcome" are an open-palmed gesture implying, "Of course, we are two decent people and we have interacted." "You're welcome", acknowledges that we've had an intentional caring exchange.

But, when we say, "No problem," it seems to mean, "I don't care if you noticed my kindness or not; I had no intention of acknowledging you as a person; if my actions came across as something nice to you, oh well." "No problem" is a closing rather than opening; it is a turning away rather than a turning toward. "No problem" is, in fact, a very real problem in relating to others.

Do these few words really make a difference? You may wish to think about it. I thank you for reading this and giving it your thought.

And now you say....

Sunday Night Feeling

If you are reading this paper on Sunday afternoon it may have already begun. You may feel its first symptom, the subtle wave of gloom spreading across your day. The cause of this feeling? No, not the weather or the flu. This is the start of "Sunday Night Feeling," an odd combination of agitation and malaise, not quite depression but a kind of dismay.

You are not alone. And it's not new. There's historic precedent for Sunday melancholy. In medieval times Sunday was a holy day with pageants and public feasts and no work. With the Reformation, Luther knocked the fun out of Sunday; there was still no work, but holiness became a kind of labor. Protestantism made Sunday a full day of worship and study.

English settlers brought that Sunday custom to our shores. In 1610, in Virginia, all you could do on Sunday was go to church and study the catechism. It was law; the penalty for a first offense was loss of a week's food; for the second, whipping; and, for the third, death. We may have lightened up over time, but the Sunday "blue laws" --named for the blue paper they were written on-- are not gone from our consciousness. Every Sunday somewhere in the United Sates it's still illegal to barber, bowl, play bingo, billiards or cards, gamble or sell alcohol or cars.

The biggest ingredient in Sunday night feeling is regret. Once again the weekend did not live up to our expectations. All week we were craving leisure and looking forward to the weekend, but what we experience is the collision of two American values: freedom and work. We keep thinking that we can work our way to freedom, but the Sunday night feeling belies the truth.

Sunday night is the start of our frenzied roller-coaster ride. This night we pull out of the station; the cable engages, chug-a-chug-a-chug; Monday morning we crest the hill and crash into the week's wild ride: commuting, committees, decisions, difficult people, office politics. For five days it's just a matter of style. You may close your eyes, grip the bar in terror, or throw up your arms and laugh. Each day there are wild swings and sharp corners, and that last whipping curve feels like a surprise each time. Then, Friday, it slows again…chug-a-chug-a-chug…Freedom!

But suddenly it's Sunday again and it feels way too soon to be back in that car.

That stomach-dropping feeling stops being fun by the 100th ride. No wonder people are drinking, fighting and playing online. At about six o'clock on Sunday night, when the anxiety about the upcoming week starts to gnaw, we want off this ride. But the credit card bills and news about the economy are the bar that holds us in our seats.

Even those of us who like our jobs have this feeling.

This is why Sunday night TV is so popular. We watch the big made-for-TV movies, the tear-jerkers and bad reality TV. We want distraction from what will come with the alarm we set so reluctantly tonight.

This is not all in your head. Monday is dreadful: Half of all illnesses begin on Monday; Monday is the busiest day in hospital emergency rooms; and most distressing, of all seven days of the week, Monday has the highest rate of suicide.

So maybe instead of gearing up on Sunday night, we should wind down. Maybe we could turn off the TV, and plan to get up earlier. Maybe Monday should be the dress-down day. Maybe we could go more gently into this good week.

Time Management

Time is not a neutral subject in my life. It is woven deeply in the fabric of my family. My father was an industrial engineer, a "time and motion study man," who carried a clipboard and wore an elegant gold Hamilton watch. I now wear that watch.

So when I make my daily to-do list, my father's ghost is nearby. I love to read about managing time and I've tried all the systems: Filofax, Day-Timer and Franklin-Covey. When I see friends tapping at their Palm Pilot and Handspring personal digital assistants, I feel the desire rise in me again. My inner voice cajoles "If you had a PDA, your life would be under control." But when I look closer and when I listen in, I do not see lives getting easier.

I know the arguments of those who have moved from planners and calendars to the PDA. I am easily assuaged by the promise of doing more and being better organized. But I resist.

I worry if I am being a technophobe. Part of my reluctance to use a PDA is that I am "haptic," one who prefers texture and who learns by touch. Friends ask why I go to the newsstand each day; "Don't you know you can read the paper online?" But I can't read a newspaper on a screen. I need to turn the pages and feel the paper. People who read a paper or magazine after me see my haptic trail...the underlining and little stars and check marks in the margin.

But the real reason I have not converted is that I still question the premise of the PDA. People who love their "digital assistants" brag about being able to carry an entire phone directory everywhere they go. I don't see that as a positive.

There is a cost created by each new technology, which corresponds to any advantage delivered. Unlimited memory makes me think I have unlimited options. Being able to carry around everyone's phone number makes me think I should be in touch with everyone all the time. Those are the kind of expectations that makes life feel more unmanageable, not less.

Sally Helgesen in her new book Thriving in 24/7, describes these hidden costs of timesaving technology. The electric washing machine, which was supposed to save time, instead increased our expectation for having cleaner clothes. When we washed by hand, we wore everything longer. Now, thanks to improved technology we are in fact spending more time doing laundry. Similarly, as we all know, cell phones, which first seemed to free us from the tether of the phone, now bind us to its constant availability. PDAs do carry lots of info, but they create an expectation that we can do so much more. The end result is not a life, just a big to-do list.

Being my father's daughter, I've had a to-do list since I was a little girl. Many years ago I got a hint that it was out of control when my ex-husband wrote on my ever-present list, "Inhale, exhale, inhale, exhale." That may be one reason why he's the Ex-husband, but he did have a point.

Having a device that can make my to-do list faster makes me think that I could, should, must do so much more.

The truth is I don't want to remember more, I want fewer things to remember. Most of us don't need to manage time better, but just the opposite: we need to relax our constant vigilance of time.

The price of that vigilance is constant anxiety.

Our insistence that time is manageable is both noble and futile. We are like the toddler standing on the beach who commands the waves, "Again, again" and watches the ocean obey.

Listen to how we talk on a busy day: "I can barely catch my breath."

Maybe the answer was on my old list after all: Inhale. Exhale.

Building Fires and Digging Wells

It is always interesting to watch the world away from home. This past week I have been in Massachusetts and watching the news from a motel room and talking to strangers about current events. Reading another town's daily papers, I see national events differently, and local stories are simultaneously more removed and more compelling in their familiar anonymity. So many difficult things happen to so very many people.

I followed the two big stories, the Middle East and the Catholic Church. Each one in its way is challenging our belief in goodness and God.

I also had time to walk on the beach this week. The ocean is always my thinking place. At the beach I am palpably aware of God and mysterious forces greater than me and the fact that history is longer than my tiny lifetime. The ocean always, and instantly, puts me in my place.

My own family has always been the lens through which I look at the world's pain. Mine was a family that could, at best, be described euphemistically as dysfunctional. But it was also a family that was deeply committed to service and community. This conjunction left me with an interesting skill set: compassion, empathy and great calm in a crisis.

The mixed blessing from my family is that I am attracted to, and ultimately skilled at easing pain. But because I am too squeamish for nursing and too impatient for teaching, I do my part by bringing resources to those who do the more skillful work of directly helping others.

Having been raised by people in pain, I know something about the different kinds of chaos a family can experience. I also know that we coped and I survived because of caring people and many kinds of help. Neighbors, churches, schools, and community organizations supported my family. So much of it was invisible.

What I know most of all is that all of us owe a debt to others. Even those who grew up in a seemingly small subset of functional families, and even those with means of every kind, have those advantages as a result of someone who came before them. My favorite quote says this very thing: "We have all drunk from wells we did not dig and been warmed by fires we did not build."

It is true; so many of the things we enjoy, pride ourselves on and sometimes take credit for, represent debts owed to people before us. We pay that debt by service, charity or simple kindness.

This column has been a place for me to build small fires every Sunday and a place to ask questions, challenge common beliefs and to ask "What if?" Now I am taking some of that fire and committing it to new work. Next week I will become the Executive Director at Community Caregivers, an organization that recruits volunteers and trains them to help neighbors in need. It's a way to ensure a deep well and a good fire for the next families.

There's a saying in 12-step programs that "Service is gratitude in action." There are many ways to serve. Some of us do it in our day jobs, others through charitable giving, some with volunteer work, and some times, most profoundly, by keeping a compassionate heart. Even children, young ones, can learn this.

Walker Percy wrote: "You can get all A's and still flunk life." That kind of failure is mostly about a lack of service.

Today, as you finish reading your Sunday paper, will you do more than shake your head at our world? As you move from whatever fire currently warms you, or protects your family, be sure to add another log for those who will follow you.

Acknowledgements:

For many years I have been helped and held by friends, family and angels. I want to thank them for the love, support and guidance that allows me to live and to have a writing life.

My love and thanks to: David Pascone, Mary Fetting, Nancy Kowalczyk, Brigid Globensky, Susan Griffiths, Stephen Cope, Kathleen Hensel, Myles Schwartz, Kathy Catlin, Diane Segal, Stephanie Gibson, Meg Tipper, Elizabeth Kirby Walsh, Jim McGrath, Betsy Voss, Leslie Ellis, Joann Crupi, Susan Cheever, Lucy Grealy, Doug Bauer, Marguerite Tierney, Sven Birkirts, Marion Roach Smith, Mary Scanlan, Peter Cameron, Judy Barnes, Kitty Hanley, Pat Dinkelaker, Marvin Freedman, Annie Decker, Mike Breslin, Johnel Bushell, Rob Kanigel, Greg Spencer, Dave Stevens, Diva de Loayza, Don Stauffer, Armand Garofalo, Eric Overmyer, Lawrence Oklota, and special thanks to Erma and Anthony.